The Joy of Solo Sex

by Dr. Harold Litten

ISBN 0-9626531-4-4

FACTOR PRESS
Post Office Box 8888
Mobile, AL 36689

INTRODUCTION

Although I've written 12 books and many hundreds of articles, I must tell you that this has been the most satisfying and rewarding undertaking of my life. The reviews were uniformly glowing. *The Book Reader* said, "In a day when everyone is uptight, when honesty is the best policy, when one must consider safety, this enlightening book will appeal to those who say, 'I'd rather do it myself, thanks.'" *Centaur* said, "Let me tell you for sure— you'll enjoy this book. It's priced right, it's funny, it's erotic, and it explores a lot of thing that you never realized..."

But more satisfying to me personally were the hundreds of letters I received from readers telling me what *Solo Sex* has meant to them. Many thanked me for showing them how to let go of senseless shame and guilt, and helping them to recognize the goodness—even sacredness of the body and its sexuality.

One of my favorite letters came from a professor in the northeast. He called the book "a scientific, devotional text by the world's leading apostle of auto-eroticism." I can think of many worse epitaphs to have engraved on my tombstone!

I hope you, too, will find pleasure and insight through the third edition of this book.

Fondly,

HAROLD LITTEN

The Joy of Solo Sex

by Dr. Harold Litten

Originally published as:
Solo Sex: Advanced Techniques

First Edition, first printing: 1990
second printing: 1991
Second edition: 1992
Third edition, as
The Joy of Solo Sex: 1993

CONTENTS

Part I The Basics

Part II Advanced Practices

Part III Ultimate Orgasm and the Mind

Part One

THE BASICS

Chapter 1
In Praise of Solo Sex

A NEW York City accountant, now in his mid 30's, tells this story:

> Late at night, Neil Henning and I, both 12 years old, huddled in our tent around an illegal kerosene lamp eating chips. We were on a Boy Scout camp-out and were talking about how babies were made. Neil doubted it. "My folks would never do that kind of stuff," he said. "Well, my father, maybe—but never my Mom."
>
> But Neil knew something that I didn't, and it was more immediately important than how babies were made. It had to do with those wet dreams I'd been having and that feeling.
>
> That was the really important stuff, so I asked Neil, "Can you get the feeling without putting it in a girl?"
>
> He laughed. Neil knew all about it. But for once he was reluctant to boast of his

knowledge. For one thing, he was ashamed. For another, he was my friend. It would kill him to watch me deteriorate into a vegetable once I became addicted.

"Swear you won't do it," he demanded, "or else you could die—or even go blind!"

I swore that I would never, ever do it, so he told me. The next day I promptly locked myself in my room, dropped my pants, took my pinky-length penis between thumb and index finger an clumsily rubbed it until the feeling shattered me.

Those minutes transformed me. It was like hearing the voice of God. The orgasm was sacred. My formerly shameful penis immediately replaced Neil as my best friend. I lavished it with time and attention. Since then it has been my constant companion, not merely as an alternative to a human partner, but for its own sake, another rich and dazzling color in the glorious spectrum of sexual joy.

Forty years ago, the belief that "you could die—or even go blind" was common. The tragedy is that even today sex therapists everywhere throughout America (although not so commonly in Europe) know first-hand the guilt that many millions of us associate with sex in general, and with solo sex in particular. We weren't born with a sense of shame about fondling our most touchable appendages. On the contrary, all infants, both male and female, play with their genitals, and some pediatricians insist that they even achieve orgasms. No, babies aren't born ashamed of doing what comes naturally.

Sexual shame is something that is learned from our parents, who in turn learned it from theirs. Your father masturbated, and so did your grandfather, for the same reasons that you do—it feels just marvelous. But they came away from each experience feeling filthy, evil, so low that they felt they could crawl under a worm's belly wearing a top hat.

That's because they were forced to read "scientific" reports like Samuel Tissot's. In 1758, Tissot published a monograph on the side-effects of masturbation, including muddleheadedness, tuberculosis, rheumatism, headaches, pimples, blisters, itching, sterility, impotence, premature ejaculation, gonorrhea, priapism (prolonged painful erection), bladder tumors, intestinal disorders, constipation, hemorrhoids and more.

Our fathers believed all that. So did millions of other guys. Yet, addicted to the feeling, they kept right on surrendering to their desires, convinced, no doubt, that they and billions of other young men like them would begin dropping dead like flies all over the world.

I have wondered seriously many times just how far emotional damage caused by this sex-negative societal indoctrination might have extended. How many millions of young men, torn on the one hand by their God-given passion for orgasm and on the other by the self-loathing which accompanied every act of self-pleasuring, ended up despising themselves, seeing themselves as dirty failures before God, chronically frightened that other humans might discover how depraved they really were.

I do not think it far-fetched in the least to suggest that, among those with sensitive consciences, such self-torture can lead to the denial of conscience entirely and ultimately the most heinous, sexually brutal crimes.

Fortunately, we've come a long way since the days when solo sex was noisily condemned. To be sure, the orthodox, or fundamentalist, elements in Protestantism, Roman Catholicism and even Judaism still specifically condemn masturbation as sinful. But they're not quite so vocal about it lately, since many studies during the past half century have shown that virtually everyone is doing it; what's to be gained by condemning those who are putting the money in the offering plates?

Those studies into the extent of solo sex began with Alfred Kinsey, who interviewed thousands of men in the 1940's, and concluded that 95 percent masturbated. In the 1960's, William Masters and Virginia Johnson raised that figure to 99 percent. But many years earlier, the eminent psychoanalyst Wilhelm Stekel didn't bother hedging his bets when he said bluntly that there is no exception to the rule that everyone pleasures himself sexually.

The same point is made in the medical tome *Masturbation From Infancy to Senescence* published by International Universities Press and edited by Irwin Marcus, M.D., and John Francis, M.D. Babies do it, say these experts. So do little boys and girls, adolescents, husbands, wives, older men and women. You and I.

Solo sex is good, clean fun. But it's much more than that, too. It's a crucial plank in the Great Plan of the Universe. Why else would the penis be located so conveniently at the junction of our thighs, equally accessible to left-handers and right, even to the feet of any flexible young man into acrobatics?

In fact, it's the focal point of the body, instantly available for detailed self-inspection, admiration an inspiration. (Any man who says he's not turned on by the sight of his own rigid penis is either lying or in need of therapy.)

Consider its size, shape and texture—a miracle of design for interludes with the hand; sufficiently short that a mere flick of the wrist is all that's needed; thick enough to provide substance, yet thin enough to permit a full grasp; arching upward to fit naturally into the shape of the palm.

Solo sex is also brilliantly practical:

You'll never catch a venereal disease making out with yourself.

You won't make anyone pregnant (as though that worry has been keeping you awake nights).

The price is right.

Even if you're under the age of consent, there's no law against having sex with yourself. (Not yet anyway, although they'll probably end up taxing it.)

According to sex researchers Dr. William Masters and Virginia Johnson, solo sex provides a more intense orgasm than any other sex act.

It's exquisitely convenient. Back in the eighth grade, we youngsters enjoyed watching Ron Mosser play with his organ behind his desk.

And he enjoyed it, too.

Millions of us have caressed ourselves while driving, walking, dining, dancing, talking on the telephone—and I certainly hope you'll do it while reading this book later on. We've done it on buses and airplanes, in forests, on rooftops and dark street corners. The country, from New

York to California, Maine to Florida, has been bathed with evidence of our joy.

Granting the above, why are most males still reluctant to admit that they masturbate—and that they love doing it?

"Only when my girl is away or not in the mood, then maybe I'll do it," says a 22-year-old straight A square student at Lehigh University in Bethlehem, Pennsylvania.

"No, I don't do it much—I prefer a guy," says a Philadelphia technician.

And so it goes, even though millions of us know very well that there are days when we can't wait to drop our pants and take hold of it.

"Masturbation is often viewed defensively as substitute behavior for something 'better,'" says Diane Brashnear, Ph,D., a marriage and sex counselor from Indianapolis, Indiana. Writing in a special report called *Honk! If You Masturbate!* For the Sex Information and Education Council of the US. (SIECUS), Dr. Brashnear argues that "the concept that self-pleasure can of itself be acceptable and positive seems wanting." We're taught to think that sexual selfishness is a sin, but, says Dr. Brashnear, "Self-pleasuring and its accompanying fantasies can be a rich experience in an otherwise tedious existence."

Washington, DC., psychiatrist Walter R. Stokes, M.D., put it this way: "I have arrived at the view, after a lifetime of clinical experience with sexual problems, that the time has come not only to throw out all the traces of our ancient negative ideas about masturbation, but boldly and unequivocally to defend it and give it the important affirmative position it should have...

"I feel we owe it to young people to give our frank and warm endorsement of auto-erotic pleasure as a completely desirable and acceptable end in itself..."

Solo sex isn't a substitute for anything, it's an end itself. Dr. Earl Marsh calls it "one of the saviors of the human race!" and Karl Kraus, Viennese writer and critic, goes so far as to proclaim that "coitus is but a weak substitute for masturbation."

The first step in getting more out of solo sex, in raising self-pleasuring to an art, is to face yourself eye to eye in the mirror and admit that you love playing with your equipment. That self-acceptance will open the door to uninhibited exploration into the full spectrum of autoerotic riches.

Now, you are gong to discover—and here is my promise to you—that this is the most honest, down-to-earth book on solo sex that you've ever read. I'll take you in hand (please forgive the pun) and lead you to experience highs which you've probably not thought possible much less enjoyed. But, as you'll learn if you don't know it already, the highest plateaus of sexual pleasures are a function not of the penis or the testicles, but of the most important sex organ of all—the brain.

That isn't just a curious fact. It's foundational to all that will follow. So get it clear now: Your brain is your most important sex organ.

If your head isn't where it ought to be—if your attitude toward solo sex isn't 100 percent positive—you can still look forward to solitary sexual pleasure that's richer, more varied and considerably more intense than you've ever known. But the most intense experiences, the multiple orgasms, and true altered state of being, require complete emotional and psychological embracing of all aspects of your sexual self.

In nearly a quarter of a century of professional experience, I've found that virtually every one of us on some level harbors sexual tensions. We can easily recognize those who are consciously guilty: they cross their legs in public, wear baggy clothes, sometimes have difficulty making eye contact with others, avoid conversations in which sex is discussed. In extreme cases, they constantly confess their sins, wash or shower several times a day. They're hiding from their sexuality, denying their genitals, attempting to scrub away their desires.

Far more common are those who suffer an unconscious sense of shame. Perhaps they even flaunt their sexuality, sitting with their legs widespread, wearing slacks that highlight their bulges. They enjoy strutting naked whenever an opportunity arises, and talk about sex incessantly.

Yet, although they themselves believe they're sex positive—that their attitude toward sex isn't influenced by prejudice, religious indoctrination or old-fashioned social values—they can be helped to confront the truth in short order:

When a man, usually in his mid-20's, approaches me with a sexual problem that is obviously emotional in nature, I will often say to him, "I'm going to ask you a series of questions, and I want you to respond instantly, without reflection." Here are a few of the questions I ask:

How would you feel if your mother knew you masturbated?

If your best buddy asks you to masturbate him to orgasm, would you?

Why or why not?

Excluding the use of force and coercion, have you ever had a sexual experience that you're ashamed of?

In interpreting the answers to these questions, I make a distinction between embarrassment and honest-to-God shame. Since I'm going to ask you right now to answer these questions for yourself, let me explain the distinction:

Embarrassment is what you feel when you're cheerfully standing at the bathroom sink, watching yourself stroke your proudly erect 16-year-old penis, when your mother throws open the door you were certain you'd locked.

Shame is what you feel after the thrill that had set your body to trembling subsides, and, although no other human being will ever know that you'd just jerked off, you still feel disgusted with yourself.

Embarrassment is your reaction to how others feel. Shame is the reaction of your own conscience. Everyone has felt embarrassment, or ought to have, since we can learn from it how to care less about peer pressure and have more confidence in ourselves.

Shame is different. It attacks our self-esteem, our very worth as people. Sexual shame can cripple our erotic functioning, allowing us only the circumspect pleasures permitted by those holding the keys to our conscience. Many millions of those so crippled have no idea how limited their sex lives are—in a world of the color blind, how would anyone know what brilliant hues and shades exist?

It's beyond the scope of this book to treat sexual shame, but for those readers who know they have a problem in this area, I recommend reading the final chapter of this book now. Understanding the origin of shame can go a long way toward dispelling it.

THE JOY OF SOLO SEX

I'm writing for readers who are comfortable with their sexuality, whether they're straight, gay or bisexual. The case histories I present will include men who represent each of those sexual identities. Readers who are secure and comfortable in their own sexual identities will not object to this. Those who are uncomfortable reading of the experiences of men whose sexual preferences differ from theirs need to explore their own sexual compulsions more honestly.

I make no apologies for viewing solo sex as good, clean wholesome fun blessed by God and prescribed by many physicians of both mind and body for health and well-being. Nor do I apologize for presenting in detail means whereby self-pleasuring, like many other invigorating forms of recreation, can be made more enjoyable. Let those bigots who have been informed by God that sex is evil challenge our right to enjoy our bodies as intensely as we are able. That evil exists I have no doubt—they've created it in their impure minds. And I believe, quite apart from theology, that damnation is theirs as well: the burning damnation of desires which they are condemned to deny.

Humana non sunt turpia—what is human, what is natural, is not harmful or evil. That ancient Roman maxim is as true today as it was when first uttered.

The conflict is simply this: the noisy minority of the many Christian sects have always condemned all sexual pleasure for the obvious reason that most people might find it much more pleasurable and fulfilling that the preacher's rantings. In fact, we need both physical and spiritual fulfillment. One cannot take the place of the other. For most people, the most wonderful sex life won't fill their spiritual needs, nor—as many religious leaders, both priests and preachers have discovered—will the most dedicated spiritual life fulfilled our sexual yearnings.

So, as you read the following pages, relax completely. Learn to handle your cock and balls with love, pride and awe, for, in the pleasure they bring, they represent a miracle, a mystery, well beyond explanation. In the following pages you'll learn how to achieve the ultimate pleasure.

When George Burns, at age 95, appeared on the *Tonight Show* in November, 1991, host Johnny Carson asked,

"When did you first get interested in girls, George?"

"I didn't [as a teen-ager]," Burns answered. "I just did it myself—didn't need anybody else. Of course in the last few years I've been wearing a glove...I believe in safe sex."

Chapter 2
How Much Is Too Much?

HERCULES DEFLOWERED 50 virgins in a single night. Proculus raped 100 women in 15 days. Antiochus, a Syrian slave, made it with 50 women in succession. Such is the stuff of which myths are made. And, while a thousand years ago, a robust sex life was considered heroic and even a special blessing of the gods, today it might well earn for you such titles as sex maniac, satyr or a victim of manic compulsive psychosis.

It seems that human existence might well be defined as a phenomenon in which one portion of the population is forever telling the other portion what is right and what Is evil and wrong, what is normal and abnormal, what is acceptable and unacceptable, what is healthy and sick. The fact is that we are no two of us alike. We differ in size, shape, in skin and hair color, in our preferences for food, entertainment, physical activity, reading, creating, sex partners—and the amount of sexual activity we want and need.

According to sexologists William Masters and Virginia Johnson, most of us have an average of about three orgasms a week. Yet, many normal, healthy men have one orgasm or less a week, and at the other extreme, some have 28 or more. Those in the "supercharged" category are usually between the ages of 20 and 40, but there are many exceptions. Some boys reach their sexual peak in their mid-teens, while there are men in their 70's who are as sexually active as guys half their age.

As I hope we've learned regarding skin color, nationality and gender, we ought certainly to learn with regard to human sexuality: being in a majority group doesn't make one right, better or of more value; being in a minority group doesn't make one wrong, less valued or less important. The rare man who reported to Masters and Johnson that he'd had 35 orgasms a week—five a day—for many years was not therefore a sicko, anymore than was the man who had only one orgasm a month.

Is there such a thing as too much sex? Masters and Johnson wrote in their classic *Human Sexual Response:*

"Every male questioned expressed a theoretical concern for the supposed mental effects of excessive masturbation, and in every case 'excessive levels' of masturbation, although not defined specifically, were considered to consist of a higher frequency than did the reported personal pattern. One man with a once-a-month masturbatory history felt once or twice a week to be excessive.

"...The man with the masturbatory history of two or three times a day wondered whether five or six times a day wasn't excessive and might lead to a 'case of nerves.'"

The fact is that, in and of itself, there is no such thing as too much sex. Whether erotic pleasures are shared with another, or focus on autoeroticism, sexuality is an appetite like that for food. Some people might require three large meals daily, while others seem to hardly eat at all. And when their appetites are satisfied, they each turn from the table to pursue other interests.

Not only is sex in any amount harmless—it's really good for you. For one thing, it can help to assure a continuing sex life into old age. A study by Clyde Martin, PhD., of the Gerontology Research Center in Baltimore, has found that men who were very active sexually in their youth stayed active; those who were not failed to have an active sex life in old age. To quote the cliche, "Use it or lose it."

Even in our everyday functioning, here and now, sex plays a crucial role—some would say the primary role—in maintaining our emotional equilibrium. Psychologist David Cole Gordon writes in his book *Self-Love*:

> Man is never more unified than during orgasm. His mind is totally quiescent at climax whether it is obtained as a result of normal heterosexual intercourse, homosexual activity or masturbation. And, as with all of his other unification experiences, he seeks to repeat them as often as possible. It should be reemphasized here that the unification experienced is [likely] so profoundly satisfying not just because man becomes one with himself, but because he also becomes one with the world and others, and for that brief moment in eternity all of his earthly problems are resolved.

Far from causing emotional distress, orgasms—as many as are desired—actually relieve it.

An active sex life can also contribute to the qualities required for professional achievement. Allen B. of Newark,

New Jersey, discovered the joys of solo sex at the age of 12, married at 20 and had sex with his wife on average twice a day and with himself one more time each day for 10 years—about 14,000 orgasms before age 30 according to his own calculations. He admits that he has always loved sex more than any other pleasure.

"Just sitting here thinking about getting turned on turns me on," he says. "My belly starts to tingle. My dick starts stretching out. I start breathing fast. You know what it is? It's the feeling of being really alive."

Allen says he's always conscious of his sexuality at work, on the subway, having dinner with his family. That doesn't mean he's always interested in sex, only that he's always aware that he's a sexual human being. As we'll see later, that sexual consciousness can lift us to a higher level of being, a much more rich, alert, alive awareness of the excitement that life can hold. And of course it will lead us into a more sexually active and pleasure-filled existence.

That's what it did for Allen. But was that too much sex? Not at all. Allen has found the time and energy to become a wealthy investor in resort properties, and some of the skeptics would find it ironic that he believes the drive and aggressiveness necessary for his success came directly from his active sex life and sex consciousness.

Several studies by endocrinologists support Allen's view. They show that sexual activity produces an increase in blood levels of the male hormone testosterone, and testosterone is essential to a sense of emotional well-being, energy, aggressiveness and perseverance—all associated with success in the business world.

"Well," say the skeptics, "that's all well and good, but once a man gets married, he should concentrate on screwing and forget about jerking off. At that point it becomes excessive."

Even half a century ago, that point of view was held primarily by men with little education. Alfred Kinsey found that fewer than one in three married men who never went to high school admitted to masturbating. Among high school graduates, 42 percent confessed to playing with themselves. But 70 percent of college graduates said they enjoyed autoeroticism even after marriage. And David Cole Gordon considers even those figures too low:

> It is suspected that masturbation among married men is more common than the statistical data indicates. It is self-evident that men when queried hesitate to admit that they have masturbated after marriage without qualifying their admission. There are in addition some men who engage in self-stimulation as a means of adding sexual variety to their lives and who continue to masturbate regardless of the amount of sexual intercourse they may have.

Howard and Martha Lewis, who offer sexual advice via computer to a growing clientele, recently received this question: 'Is there something wrong with me? I'm an 18-year-old guy, and I find that I usually enjoy masturbating more than having sex with my girlfriend."

The experts explained that masturbation often provides more intense pleasure than intercourse "because an individual can concentrate entirely on personal sensations, without having to think about a partner's needs. One can let go and self-centeredly enjoy sexual feelings." Other

19

factors involving sex with another person include the desire for privacy along with performance anxiety, fear of pregnancy and disease.

Writing in *Medical Aspects of Human Sexuality*, Donald W. Hastings, M.D., of the University of Minnesota Medical School, says, "Masturbation is common in married men and has no particular significance. It is a common misconception that masturbation stops upon marriage and that if it occurs after it, the man must be suffering from an emotional disturbance. Neither of these ideas is true."

Solo sex as part of the erotic life of a married man does not constitute too much sex.

Yet, there is indeed the possibility of having too much sex—and it's important that you know about it. It's not the frequency, but the compulsion to have sex that might suggest a problem—and that's true whether the sex is with a man, a woman, or yourself. The man who shares love and sexual fulfillment with his lover, yet must continually add notches to his belt with new sex partners, thereby risking the relationship he cares about, has no less compulsive a sexual problem than, say, the air traffic controller who can't keep his mind and hands out of his pants whether or not planes are arriving and departing on the same runway. Only when solitary sex begins interfering with relationships and responsibilities, when it becomes compulsive, is there a problem—and then the problem isn't with autoeroticism but with other conflicts.

The eminent Psychoanalyst Dr. Krafft-Ebing describes such a man: "D. was compelled at times, when his sexual excitement was excessive, to perform the sexual act from 10 to 18 times in 24 hours..."

That's 70 to 105 orgasms a week. But it's not the numbers alone that led Dr. Krafft-Ebinq to rightly diagnose his patient's behavior as satyriasis. (In Greek mythology, satyrs, half human and half horse or goat, were credited with fantastic sexual endurance and appetite.) It wasn't the amount of sex that was D.'s problem but the compulsion that drove him to it—the fact that he had all those orgasms "without deriving any feeling of satisfaction."

The satyr, according to Frank S. Caprio, M.D., is a man who "suffers from an excessive craving for sexual relations" but whose "libido is never gratified."

A healthy male is sexually aroused, engages in sex, reaches orgasm, experiences complete satisfaction and fulfillment, perhaps rests if he is alone or shares some pleasant afterplay with his partner, and typically goes on to other pursuits—unless, of course, he has deliberately devoted the day or the weekend to erotic pleasure. The satyr or sex addict knows no such resolution of his lust, no fulfillment. For the satyr, sex is like an itch that, no matter how hard he tries, he can't scratch.

After a few years, Krafft-Ebing's patient, D., stopped having sex with his wife, relying instead exclusively on masturbation. He averaged three orgasms daily, but they were seldom fulfilling. Sex was constantly on his mind.

D. was a high school teacher, and one day he got turned on just looking at one of the well-built girls in his classroom. With a desk protecting him from his students' eyes, D. unzipped his pants and masturbated to an orgasm so intense that it was obvious to everyone. It was a mistake that cost D. his job and almost landed him in jail.

Yet he could not have helped himself. He needed not just sex, but sexual fulfillment.

Dr. Patrick Carnes, a Minneapolis psychologist and author of the book *The Sexual Addiction*, says that one in 12 adults in this country, like D., are sex addicts, with perhaps two-thirds of them being men. Predictably, the most common activity among them is solo sex—Carnes tells of a businessman who was so obsessed with sex that he locked himself in the men's room several times a day while at work so that he could masturbate.

The sure sign that sex is becoming compulsive —an addiction—is that it begins interfering with other aspects of life. Richard B. Lower, M.D., of the University of Pennsylvania Medical School, tells of three college students who came to him for help because, although they were of superior intelligence, they were failing academically. Each finally admitted that he couldn't concentrate on studying because he was sexually obsessed, masturbating 10 to 12 times a day.

"For most sexual compulsives," writes sex researcher George Whitmore, "excessive sexual behavior accomplishes not a lessening but an intensification of tension and anxiety. Relief is harder to achieve and more fleeting. Once is certainly not enough—soon 100 times wouldn't be."

Writing in *The Advocate*, Whitmore tells the story of Jack, a gay man who found himself in a subway toilet at four o'clock in the afternoon after having stopped there on his way to work that morning. "I hadn't eaten all day, and I hadn't called the office because I didn't want to take the time out from sex."

Because of stories like this—and others about gay promiscuity—there's a tendency to associate sexual obsession with homosexuality. In fact sexual addiction is by no means an exclusively gay phenomenon. Albert Eliis, PhD., writes in *Human Autoerotic Practices*, "Any kind of sexuality, including normal intercourse, can get performed compulsively. I, too, have seen several women who feel they kept getting driven 'up the wail' by their partners' compulsively insisting that they achieve orgasm in various ways..."

Even Dear Abby recently quoted the wife of a 44-year-old sexually compulsive man: "My problem is that this man is insatiable in the bedroom. He's been this way ever since we married. He wants sex at least three times a day. On weekends we spend the whole day in bed. I thought he would eventually slow down but his sex drive is as strong as ever."

In fact, Richard C. Pillard, M.D., of the Department of Psychiatry at Boston University Medical School, says that the record number of orgasms among his patients is 21 in three days—and it was set by a compulsive heterosexual.

The man who is truly addicted to sex, says Dr. Carnes, will recognize that he is powerless over his sexual addiction and that it has made his life unmanageable. That's the first step in Dr. Carnes's treatment program, now adapted in varying degrees by hundreds of organizations involving thousands of people all over the country.

Pete is typical of the men who attend Carnes' meetings, He married shortly after graduation, had an excellent sex life with his wife, yet found his desire for sex increasing as the pressures of his job grew greater. He began peeking into bedroom windows, masturbating in his car as women walked by. Finally, he exhibited himself to a passing woman during orgasm and ejaculation.

"One spring day," says Carnes, "he had the peak exhibitionist experience. A young woman had put her head in the window of the car, talked to him and watched him masturbate to ejaculation." When he returned home, he found a police officer waiting for him.

How much sex is too much? Any amount that's compulsive, that interferes with other aspects of your life, or that requires taking illegal risks in order to reach fulfillment.

Apart from that, no amount is too much—unless, of course, you flog yourself raw. As sexologist Albert Ellis, PhD., points out in *Human Autoerotic Practices*, edited by Manfred F. DeMartino, young men in particular usually have considerably more sexual potential than they actually use. Writes Ellis, "You will find it almost impossible to masturbate to excess, unless you turn practically psychotic —because erotic response depends upon a remarkably foolproof mechanism. When you reach the limit of your physiological endurance, you no longer respond sexually."

Even if you give it your best shot—as a World War II prisoner was forced to do in a German Concentration camp—you probably don't have anything to worry about. Ellis quotes Professor Douglas Sprenkle, who relates that the Germans forced the prisoner to masturbate every three hours, 24 hours a day, for two years as part of an experiment on human potency. When the soldier was released, the physicians found no evidence of physical damage or emotional trauma.

Nor did the young man swear off sex. Instead he married and had a child. And no doubt continued to enjoy solo sex, too, although Sprenkle is silent on that point.

THE JOY OF SOLO SEX

The ancient Greek Philosopher Diogenes periodically masturbated in a crowded marketplace, shocking his fascinated observers. The act was not illegal, but it was certainly considered inappropriate; sex activity was then, as now, considered a private thing.

Diogenes explained his behavior by saying that any act which is natural cannot be shameful. Masturbation was merely the satisfaction of a need, and if the need arose while in public, it should be satisfied forthwith.

—Michael Foucault, *The Uses of Pleasure*

Chapter 3
An Evening Alone With You

ANSWER: "I'D rather die."

Question: How serious is a Friday night without a date?

The 20-year-old Penn State sophomore—I'll call him Joe Smith to protect him from ridicule—who gave that answer also says, "God made Friday nights for scoring. That's what it's all about."

But Joe doesn't score that often. And since the drinking age is 21 in Pennsylvania, he and his buddies rarely hit the bars on Friday nights. So, what does Joe really do when he doesn't have a date?

"I sit in my room, stuff my face with popcorn, watch some lousy TV shows and hate everybody that's out having a good time."

Most men feel the same way. Psychologist Reed Larson of the University of Chicago found that young adults are not only more likely to feel lonely than older people, but to feel it more profoundly, especially on Friday and Saturday nights when they're at home without dates.

"The culture tells us that if you're alone on Friday night you're going to be scared and miserable," says Philip Shaver, social psychologist at New York University. "No wonder young people feel that way."

Of course, young people aren't the only ones who, contrary to their wishes, find themselves alone. Just two examples, the first a middle-aged married executive:

"I have a wonderful family, a good sex life, two young sons and a job that's perfect except for one thing. I spend two weeks a month on the road. The worst part is I miss my wife and kids. Second worst is the sexual thing. I've been tempted to pick up someone, but it's not my style. And of course there's always the possibility of bringing home a disease."

Another man is in his 60's, widowed last year and lonely ever since. He explains his feelings poignantly: "I just don't seem to be enough for myself."

That's a particularly significant statement, because it's right on target with what most psychologists consider the problem of loneliness. It illustrates the low self-esteem and lack of self-love that this mature gentleman feels. But the same was true of the college student, Joe Smith, and the middle-aged businessman. For these men and millions like them, aloneness is a synonym for loneliness. Forced to be alone with themselves, they often escape into drugs and alcohol.

Taken to its extreme, that kind of desperate need to be in the presence of others, to have another person around always in order to feel complete, can actually destroy relationships and leave one more lonely than ever.

While many, and perhaps most, people can honestly say, "My very best friend in the world is me," there are millions who don't feel that way, and that's unfortunate, for when all is said and done, we live most intimately with ourselves. We spend more time with ourselves than with others, for we are always, obviously, in our own company. Ultimately, it is no one's responsibility but our own to keep us from becoming bored, to plan our lives, to entertain us. To do those things, we must love ourselves. Self-love Is critical to sound mental health.

Those who lack self-love end up having unstable relationships with others. Writes Terri Schultz in *Bitter Sweet*, "a therapist told me that the best preparation for living with somebody is to first live alone. 'If you learn to live with yourself, then you have less expectation that other people are going to provide answers for you.'"

Beyond that, we all need love. There are no two ways about it. If you can't provide that feeling of security and value as a gift from yourself to yourself, then you will demand it from friends and acquaintances. We all know such people. The main characteristic they display is the constant seeking of attention, praise and affection. Some sublimate the need for affection and attention into hyper-sexuality and come on so aggressively in terms of sex as to seem neurotic, or even pathological. What they really need is to learn to love themselves.

You should certainly be wondering by now what Joe Smith, the dateless Penn State sophomore, has in common with the middle-aged businessman, the mature widower, and all those people who do not know how to love themselves adequately—and, yes, you, who are reading this book to learn how to find greater pleasure in solo sex. The answer is that both they and you need to experience self-love if you haven't already done so. Among other things, that means learning to enjoy your own company—and what better way to do that than to date yourself?

What if Joe Smith had answered the question that introduced this chapter—How serious is a Friday night without a date?—by declaring proudly, "Friday night without a date? Impossible. I'm spending Friday night with me!"

Actually, millions of people confess to preferring their own company to that of others. Most of them are women, since men must contend with the wearisome peer group pressure which demands that we all pretend that we would prefer to slit our throats than to go to bed without a woman. In fact, that's a major reason that men have failed to develop as wholesome a sense of individual value and contentment with themselves as women have, in general.

Those who want the most from solo sex have a reason beyond that of emotional health for spending an evening alone with themselves.

The most advanced, profound solo sex experiences are in a very real sense other-worldly, something akin to a fourth dimension, and it exists not externally but internally—within yourself. While everyone is capable of ordinary masturbation, only those who enjoy their own company, and are comfortable and confident in themselves, who experience what psycho-therapists call complete unity of the self, are likely to reach that altered state of being which makes possible the ultimate orgasm.

Plan now for an evening alone with you, and consider it a first step toward your ultimate goal.

Begin by choosing a specific Friday night. Make sure you have no other commitments after you're through with school or work. Don't try to squeeze in dinner with a friend or parents first. Don't plan to stop by at Buns and Beaver Bar afterward to see what's going on. Spend the entire evening alone with yourself—and you'll look forward to it with a tingle of excitement in your gut.

Now, what would you really like to do? It's so easy to get caught up in the rat race of schedules and studies or job decisions and pressures, or pleasing others, or conforming to expectations and peer pressures. Frequently we completely lose sight of our selves. For that reason, deciding what we really want to do with the time we've devoted to ourselves might not be all that easy.

Perhaps it might be something as simple as window shopping or treating yourself to some new clothes—or both. A young editor who recently graduated from a college in Greenville, South Carolina, recalls one of the least expensive favorite self-indulgences of all time:

"The whole thing took about an hour and a half, which is a lot of time to spend on no productive purpose when you're working your way through college and taking a full load," he says. "I'd walk to town, have a leisurely vanilla milk shake, easy on the syrup and lots of ice cream, and walk back to campus. I owe my sanity, especially during my senior year, to that milk shake ritual."

Perhaps you'd like to go to dinner in an exclusive restaurant. The devil will tell you it costs too much, and you're not worth it, so tell the devil to go to hell, where he belongs. Make the reservation. Is there a film you've wanted to see? Make up your mind to do it.

Withdraw the money you'll need a few days ahead of time so that there's no last minute rushing, reconsidering or getting cold feet—as dates have been known to do.

A particularly pleasant way to spend an evening with you is to prepare a gourmet dinner at home. "I don't do it often," says Alan G., of New York City, "but once every couple of months I pick up a frozen lobster tail, a good fat one, some fresh asparagus, a bottle of champagne and go to it."

Even while in high school, Alan never had trouble getting dates. He's blond, blue-eyed, good looking, a Chris Atkins type, who draws girls the way flowers draw bees. His athletic prowess and easy nature attract male friends as well, to the point where he rarely has free time.

"I don't think I could survive mentally if i didn't just put time aside for myself," he says. "You got to keep in touch with you, stay friends with yourself, or you're no good to anyone. So, I tell everybody I'm going out of town for the weekend, take the phone off the hook and I guess you could say I have a date with myself."

If you're dining at home, go through the preparations mentally to make sure you have everything you'll need—the seasonings, the sauces, corkscrew or whatever.

During the early part of the evening, enjoy yourself thoroughly. Whatever it is that you've decided to do, do it with the wide-eyed, fun-filled enthusiasm you knew as a child. Don't worry about tomorrow or yesterday, but enjoy the moment for itself.

But regardless of what you do in the early part of the evening, eventually you'll return to the place where you'll spend the night—your room, apartment, or even a hotel room where you know you can have privacy.

Let's face it: although not always the case, dating and sex usually go together like hand and glove—or at least we'd like them to. There's no reason that shouldn't be true when you're dating yourself. After all, if you're too proud to give yourself sex, why should anyone else do it?

The most wonderful thing about being alone with you is that you finally have a partner with whom you can be completely honest about your sexual turn-ons.

Step 1. Establish the mindcast. From the moment you're awakened on the day that you've chosen, try to maintain this frame of mind: "For this one day, I'll guard against all sexual fantasies.

"I will think no thoughts having to do with sex except one—periodically, I will envision myself naked. In my mind, I will survey my body. I will realize how vulnerable I am to my sexual desires, how helpless to resist my need for orgasm. I will have the pleasure I need. It is inevitable. In my imagination, I am waiting even now, naked."

Throughout the day return to those thoughts and ambitions, heightening your anticipation of what awaits.

Step 2. Select the right setting. It will be, first of all, a place where you feel safe and secure. If it's to be your own apartment, be certain to begin days ahead of time notifying people that you will not be home. It's a little white lie that can save a great deal of embarrassment.

One young man tells what happened when he failed to do that. He was so doted upon by his parents that he finally moved out at age 22. One Friday night after work he decided to spend the entire evening in the pleasures of solo sex. He disconnected the phone to avoid any distractions and went to bed with a few artificial penises, women's lingerie and a couple of cock rings.

During the evening, his parents attempted to reach him by phone, and when they failed, they imagined the worst, raced to his apartment, to which his mother had a key, and promptly discovered that their son had become his own person in ways they'd never imagined.

The right setting is one in which you feel completely safe from intrusion, comfortable and at ease. If necessary, rent a motel room and tell no one. If possible, prepare it for your arrival ahead of time. Stash the beverages and hors d'oeuvres in the refrigerator. Have the candles and music ready. You don't want to break the mood by having to go shopping between the dinner/theater part of the evening and the erotic conclusion. (That's also a good thing to keep in mind when dating another person.)

Although erotic magazines, videos and such are perfectly fine during an ordinary solo sex session, you shouldn't use them during this evening alone with you unless you are absolutely certain that you can't get turned on any other way. The reason to avoid them is that this experience has an important secondary purpose, that of helping you to develop a higher psychic sexual intensity. You will learn to begin concentrating on yourself, on your own body and its sensations, and nothing else.

For that you will need two mirrors, one about two feet wide and three feet long, and another hand-held. Plan ahead of time to have them just where you'll need them.

Step 3. Pamper yourself. Devote the whole evening to yourself, to treating yourself lavishly. If you prefer not to go out for dinner, prepare something special at home—remember Alan's lobster tails? Again, be sure to have all the necessary ingredients already at hand.

Afterward, take a warm, leisurely soaking, a bubble bath if you like. Turn the music up and light the candles in the bathroom. Perhaps you'd like to nibble some crackers and caviar while bathing. Damn the expense. You wouldn't hesitate to order champagne and caviar if you were hoping to take a lover to bed, so why grow miserly when It's yourself with whom you're going to spend the night? In fact, there's at least one good reason for treating yourself even better than you would a date—you know that eventually you're going to come across.

Step 4. **Tease the fire.** After you've bathed and dried, powder or oil your entire body while observing yourself in the large mirror. Do not stimulate your genitals physically, and do not entertain a sex fantasy, but rivet your eyes and attention on the mirror reflection of your own body, your sex organs, allowing your desire to grow inside you.

If you can truly release yourself into this, and get thoroughly absorbed in the sexuality that permeates every part of you, it can be an experience you've never known before.

"I started breathing very fast," says one man. "I was just panting, like a dog on a hot day. I can't really put into words what was happening, just that I knew somehow, differently than I ever thought about it before, that I was totally sexual. IT WAS LIKE ALMOST BEING A SEX ORGAN FROM MY HEAD TO MY TOES. And while I stood there I started trembling, really shaking. This warm feeling came over me, like I was being bathed in the sweet softness of sex."

Don't rush it. Tease the fire. Get deeper and deeper into it.

Step 5. Play the scene. Creative men have come up with all sorts of possibilities:

"I like to put the mirror on the sofa to my right, lay on my back across an ottoman so that my abdomen arches upward and watch myself slowly caressing my own cock."

"I'm on my belly. My legs are on the sofa and my chest on a stool. I have a spotlight underneath, shining up on my cock and balls. The mirror is in front of me, aimed just at that part of my body. I just stare at it, minute after minute, concentrating on nothing but that fat, hard dick and dangling nuts. I get so hot it doesn't take much to get me off."

"I just stand there in front of the bathroom mirror and watch myself pet my own body—my chest, my abdomen. I comb my fingers through my pubic hair. Finally, I caress my balls and cock. I'm not much to look at, but when I'm making love to myself I really feel beautiful. I'm not ashamed to say I fall in love with me. I've learned that I can get hooked on my own body."

Let it all happen at its own lazy pace. Let the feeling of inevitable ecstasy fill you, overwhelm you, a tingling mini-orgasm in its own right, this full-body awareness that you're helpless to prevent the pleasure and therefore needn't rush it.

David Cole Gordon, in his book *Self-Love*, has pointed out that this sort of profound autoerotic experience has a powerful healing and strengthening effect on the psyche that is almost spiritual. Unlike the quickie orgasm, the power of a sustained, focused experience like this comes from being alone with ourselves and enjoying our company, feeling comfortable and happy with who we are and ultimately sharing great ecstasy with no one but ourselves.

The result: Successful self-pleasuring also makes us good with others and desired by them. Some people have called it character, others strength. But it's really just the high self-esteem and self-love that might well begin with an evening alone with you.

And here's something that might surprise you: once you find yourself able to look forward to evenings alone with yourself regularly, you're but a breath from the psychic orgasm.

THE JOY OF SOLO SEX

"Your body is the harp of your soul and it is yours to bring forth sweet music from it or confused sounds."

—*The Prophet*, Kihil Gabran

Chapter 4
Creative Touching

THIS CHAPTER—indeed this entire book—is written for the serious connoisseur of sex. The adolescent knows that he wants to plunge headlong to orgasm. It's new, overwhelming even metaphysical experience for him and he can't be blamed for simply clutching his phallus and beating it to ejaculation as quickly as possible. Impatience is the hallmark of youth even if it results in muscle cramp and friction burn.

Of course there are adults who maintain this adolescent approach to sex throughout their lives, beating off in the same old way day in and day out followed by the requisite guilt and shame, finally marrying, enjoying sexual intercourse only in the missionary position—man on top, woman on bottom—convinced for reasons that no one can explain that this is the way God meant it to be done, while physiologically the curvature of uterus and penis is such that rear entry is the more natural way if procreation is the objective.

And of course there are men in their teens who are sophisticated well beyond their years in sexual matters. They, like you, who are reading these words, understand that sex is like food in that one can eat to satisfy hunger and meet nutritional needs—or one can dine for the pleasure that exquisite food artfully prepared can bring.

To continue the analogy, most men, even the connoisseurs, ignore the sexual appetizers. They recognize the obvious sexual significance of their genital organs but make the error of assuming that their sexuality is entirely concentrated in six inches of erect penis and three inches of testicles (all right let s be generous: ten inches of penis and six inches of testicles). And of course erotic videos don't help to correct this misconception. Whether the partner in these flicks is a woman or another man the stereotypical—and often boring—plot is inevitably from clothed to naked to genital play to orgasm. Such films suggest that their producers see men as nothing but gonads.

In fact the entire bodies of both men and women are erotic. And I will tell you now that if you have localized your sense of sexuality to your genitals exclusively, if you think of sex merely as an affair of the cock and balls, you must break free of such limitations if you are to achieve a higher level of sexual pleasure. The altered state of sexuality which leads to ultimate pleasure requires not only an intellectual recognition but an emotional assurance that every cell of your body has its own throbbing sexual existence.

Think of the following series of exercises as the appetizers. They're designed to help you discover the most erogenous zones, the most sexually stimulating parts of your body. How important are they? First they might open the door to the generalized total body orgasm that so many women and so few men enjoy. Second some men—few to be sure—have reported completely satisfying orgasms through stimulation of an erotic part of their bodies—without any contact with the phallic area. Speak of mastering the possibilities!

You are going to caress yourself using just the balls of your fingers and a light teasing stroke. Always slide your fingers toward you. If you use your finger tips in an away stroke you'll create greater pressure and friction and the difference can break the mood of caressing.

The backs of your fingers are good for any away stroke and can even be used in flicking movements as though you're bushing off crumbs from your lap.

Your fingernails are a really wonderful tool for erotic touching. The classic *Kama Sutra,* the ancient Hindu love manual, elevates the fingernail to the status of a virtual sex organ, actually distinguishing lovers by the quality of their fingernails. The book's author, Vatsyayana, describes eight techniques for using the fingernails. He writes, "The parts of the body on which these caresses should be perpetrated are: the armpit, the throat, the breast, the lips, the jaghana (abdomen), and the thighs."

For some parts of your body you will use your entire open hand.

Begin with your feet. Lying on your back, bend one knee so that the foot of that leg rests on the opposite thigh. Very gently trace an imaginary line from the ball of your big toe across the arch or the foot to the base of the heel. Use two or three fingers with such light strokes that if anyone else were touching you it would tickle. (Theoretically it s impossible to tickle ourselves.) Continue for 30 seconds to a minute. Do you feel the sensations rush to your abdomen and groin?

Lie on your side, the upper leg straight, the bottom one bent slightly so that you can reach the back of your knee. Most women and many men find this area highly responsive to touch. Use a gentle circular motion.

The inner thighs are highly sensitive from just above the knees to the scrotum. (Remember that at this point you're to avoid intentional contact with the genitals.) Here's one technique:

Place pillows against the headboard of your bed so that you can lie back at a slightly inclined angle. Place your feet together so that the soles touch and your knees are spread wide apart. With your eyes closed (this is a tactlie exercise not a visual one) begin moving your fingers in a line along your inner thighs from your knees toward your groin. Use either a continuous or feathering stroke, very light.

About halfway to three-fourths of the way along you'll discover a sharply sensitive area. Linger there, tuning in to the sensuality of the touch.

When the stroke is complete trace it back to the knees with the backs of your fingers or fingernails.

Some people find a rougher stroke more satisfying. If you're among them use your fingernails to scrape rather than to caress. Even for those who prefer gentleness this rougher handling can sometimes provide pleasant variety.

The male torso is visually erotic—if it weren't so it would not have been the single most sculpted subject in history. It is also full of sensitive, stimulating nerves. If you haven't discovered that yet, lie on your back and use the balls of your fingers. Start at your armpit and move down your side to the bottom of your rib cage. Continue down to the last rib, then inward to the breast bone and down your abdomen to your pubic hair. Now reverse the process.

Linger at the nipples, tracing them in a circular motion, stimulating them. Some men enjoy tweaking their nipples, and there are cases on record of men having orgasms simply by lavishing their nipples with attention. That's rare, and highly eroticized nipple sensation is apparently a gift some people are born with. But many men find the nipples an erogenous zone.

On the other hand, some men have no erotic response whatsoever to nipple play. Of course that's no physical defect or problem. It's analogous to the preference for one food rather than another.

One of the most erotic and frequently overlooked touches a man can receive—either from himself or a partner—is the full-hand torso massage. For all their macho strutting, all men whether straight gay or in between, enjoy the strength of other men. That's why beer swigging truck drivers and hard-hat construction workers pay good money to be entertained by weight lifters, body builders, football players, and the less than intellectual exploits of Swartzenegger, Nolte, and Stallone. That's as close as homophobic straights will permit themselves to get to another male—a depiction on a screen. Others exper-ience man-to-man physical contact through sports in which hugging, pinning, groping, goosing, and touching are acceptable within the context of the game.

In fact one of the great tragedies of human existence is that men cannot admit their need to bond with and share the strength of other men. Instead millions of them sit in bars getting drunk all night every night in order to have masculine company. Others buy heterosexual erotica featuring the late John Holmes who, bless him, was ugly, scrawny, pot-bellied, and packed a 14-inch penis. These heterosexual men made Mr. Holmes the most popular and successful erotic performer in the history of the world not because he was a good actor (he was truly terrible) or a great screwer (he was mediocre) but because through films they could satisfy a need they dare not act upon in real life: to pay homage to another man's sexual power.

That sort of thing isn't a homosexual compulsion, it's a human one, and those men who are happiest with themselves recognize it. When it comes to sensual touching there are few feelings as pleasing to the typical male as that of a strong masculine hand moving across his chest, abdomen, navel, and pubic hair, then back up the torso in a slow, continuing motion. The touch should be firm, confident, masculine, the movement continuing slowly but without hesitation. It's a caress we can easily bestow upon ourselves for deep satisfaction.

Experiment with the less common techniques as well. Perhaps you're among those men who enjoy having his ears played with. Perhaps your throat is an erogenous area. Drop your head back over the side of the bed and brush your throat with feathery, shingling touches. Some men discover the inner point of their upper arms and armpits are highly sensitive, and caressing them gives pleasure.

It's your body. Play with it. Explore it. Enjoy it. You might be surprised to know that even in the Bible Belt self-pleasuring isn't illegal.

I spoke of the erotic auto-caress as the appetizer. To hold the analogy, the main course is phallic touching. But not just your everyday touching, variously referred to according to B. W. Von Bloch in his book *The Masturbaters,* as:

Ball Off, Beat the Dummy, Boff, Jerk Off, Pound the Meat, Diddle One's Self, Plub the Dub, Finger Fuck, Flog the Bishop, Take the Pickle, Sit on the Banana, Gallop the Antelope, Fudge, Give a Hand Job, Hand Gig, Jack Off, Jerk the Gherkin, Lope the Mule, Get it Off One's Self, Play With, Pinch the Cat, Pinch the Pussy, Choke the Dog, Pocket Pool, Pull the Pud, Work Off, Pound Off, and many, many others.

(If you're curious, Porter Davis adds, to that list in his book *Auto-erotic Practices:* "Genital Vice, Solitary Maneuver, Manual Vice...Solitary Passion, Unnatural Passion, Manual Defilement, Solitary Libertinage, Mastupration, Solitary Vice, Onan's Crime, Manustupration, Cheromana, Onanism, The Sin of Youth, Ipsation, Autoism, Autoerastia, Geistive Onanie, Monosexual Idiosyncrasy, Autophilie, etc.")

Although some of the names are exotic, all of that is your run-of-the mill stuff, what one 29-year-old who has been doing it at least once a day for a decade and a half describes this way: You take hold of it, beat it up and down. Sometimes you come up with a fantasy. Sometimes you look at pictures. That s all there is to it.

He's telling the truth—that's his own pathetically limited experience. But the variety of touch techniques in solo sex can be far more creative and stimulating than that. It can be a night at Windows on the World or the Four Seasons. And it costs nothing but the desire to shoot for something better.

The Glans Massage

"I don t grab my penis in my hand as one would hold the staff of the American flag," wrote one 42-year-old naturalized American citizen in response to an article on solo sex which I wrote some years ago for a well-known men's magazine.

"I use the tips of my fingers and hold the top part of my penis as one would pick up a pebble. I wet my penis with saliva and caress it gently by stroking it up and down, sometimes fast sometimes slowly, squeezing my fingers around the top and releasing them, going lightly around it. I don't touch myself in other places."

The object here is to concentrate attention exclusively on the glans or head of the penis. For some men, particularly those who have foreskins, the glans can be too sensitive for this technique. Particularly younger men who remain intact find the exposed glans very sensitive to direct contact. (The other side of that coin is that anecdotal evidence not scientifically verified suggests the possibility that uncircumcised men experience more intense orgasm.)

Orgasms, as you may have discovered—and certainly will in the course of reading this book—don't require direct stimulation of the penile glans. When the glans itself is stimulated as described by the man above, the sensation takes on an unusual aspect. A feeling of warmth spreads over the entire body and the tingling in the penis becomes like an itch, both pleasant and disturbing. It may continue to build until merged into the thrill of orgasm—or the disturbing sensation can become distracting until it proves unsatisfying and uncomfortable.

That s true when the glans is highly sensitive or when the friction is too forceful. Since the feeling is triggered primarily in the corona or large outer rim of the cockhead, the discomfort can be avoided by concentrating the touch on other parts of the glans.

Perhaps a better approach is to practice what another correspondent called *knob nooky:* "First I lubricate the head of my cock with a little hand lotion," he writes. "Then I take hold of the top with my fingers and twist the head left and right real quick like I'm opening and closing the lid of a jar. Don't think about anything, sex fantasies, etc. I just let myself get into the feeling. In a few minutes I either have to stop or shoot. It s pretty neat."

Slapping It Silly

You're not likely to win a race for ejaculation with this one, but, if you enjoy feeling hard and turned on for prolonged periods, this can be fun.

One approach is to simply slap your erect penis gently from side to side using both hands and maintaining a steady rhythm. Another is to lay one hand between your lower abdomen and your penis and use the backs of your fingers to slap the penis away as rapidly as it springs back.

Foreskin Fun

The greatest number and variety of nerve endings in the penis by far are located in the foreskin, making it highly sensitive to touch, temperature—and, unfortunately, pinching in zippers. (Even among masochists that all-too-common experience is not a popular thrill.) Here's how some men who have foreskins—a growing number each year now approaching 50 percent in some states—use them to increase the pleasure of solo sex.

"I have a small soft artist's brush and I like to tickle the foreskin with it all around the cockhead, just real light, you know. It's better than a tongue."

"My foreskin's very sensitive. I like to tickle it with my finger where it surrounds the head. It's a good feeling, makes me get hard quick."

Shaft Stimulation

The major function of the foreskin, other than the obvious protection it provides for the glans, is to make thrusting or insertion easier. When the foreskin is pulled forward over the glans it acts as a sleeve through which the shaft of the penis slides, thereby reducing friction between penis and vagina, or in solo sex between the shaft and the hand.

"When I play with my dick," says one man, "I make sure the foreskin's over the head of my cock. When I pull my hand down the foreskin just rolls off the head leaving it bare naked there in all it's glory. But when I slide my hand forward again, the skin comes between my hand and the head and there's no hard friction, just nice easy rolling back and forth."

Lacking foreskins, many men lubricate the glans with lotions or gels. That's a good idea to avoid discomfort and even friction burns if you plan to spend much time massaging your penile head itself. Here are some common—and not so common—strokes:

The Flog. This is the traditional five-fingered fist grip full-speed beat-off. It proceeds from the base of the penis to the head and serves the purpose of quick release. Preferred by adolescents, it isn't the usual technique of the experienced self-pleasurer.

The Head Bang. Fingers grasp the shaft as above, slide firmly to the head and strike the corona—but do not proceed over the glans, which is never directly stimulated. As a result, sensations develop slowly, heightening the emotional tension.

Bang The Balls. Here the more powerful stroke is in the downward direction. And it introduces a new and very important concept to autoerotic stimulation: *Direct contact with the glans of the penis is not necessary to produce orgasm.* In fact the most intense orgasms, the sort that seem to flow through your entire body, are most commonly achieved when the glans is not directly stimulated.

For this technique, grab the penis just beneath the corona. (Men with foreskins must pull the skin tight at the base of the penis before grasping the shaft.) Grip firmly to prevent sliding. Now tug downward in rhythmic motions so that the skin attached to the head grows taut and relaxed in rapid succession.

You needn't tug forcefully and, depending on the size of your organ, your fist will not actually move far enough down the shaft to bang your balls. The trick is to concentrate on the feeling in your penis, the growing tension, the slow oozing up of sensation building ever so patiently to orgasm.

The strokes should be short, not more than an inch, just enough to relieve the tautness of the skin and to reestablish it.

The following strokes are variations on the theme of orgasm without direct contact with the glans. If you're going to attain the ultimate orgasm, discussed later, you'll have to master one of these techniques. That's how you'll develop your capacity to reach a high level of sexual arousal through lust and concentration rather than physical stimulation alone.

Let me repeat now--and I'll surely say it again later because it is the basis of all sexuality: *Sexual pleasure is almost entirely mental, not physical.* You already know that your brain can produce sexual arousal—that's what fantasies are all about. It can also produce orgasm and ejaculation, perhaps not in all men, for it depends on the intensity of their sex drive, but certainly in many—without any physical stimulation whatever. That's what you will be conditioning yourself to experience with these delicate strokes—less reliance on the physical and more on the mental/emotional.

Two-Finger Down-Stroke. This is the same technique as the previous one except that the contact is reduced to a feathery touch on the shaft and the stroke itself is more subtle. You may want to start with the full-hand grip switching to the thumb and index finger and easing the stroke as the sensation begins building toward climax.

Shake the Head. Grasp the shaft as in *Bang the Balls* above. Pull the skin taut. Now, instead of stroking simply shake the penis very rapidly. You'll have to be at a very high level of erotic desire—really hot, to put it more plainly—to go all the way with this technique, but it's a thrilling way to finish off after building up with other strokes if you don't mind shooting sperm all over the room.

Tug the Testes. Perhaps the most sophisticated of manual (or hand) techniques, only a handful of men have actually experienced orgasm this way, although most are capable of it. It can be done in various positions.

For example, you might lie on your side, reach over your buttocks, grasp your scrotum from behind and begin tugging it rhythmically. Of course you can cheat in the beginning by using your other hand to stimulate the glans until reaching an adequate level of sexual tension. Simply keep tugging the sac until the inevitable happens.

More enjoyable for some is standing at a bathroom mirror and reaching back and behind to grasp the testes between the legs. In this position you can focus visually on the rhythmically spasming organ and yield completely to the feelings of fullness in the genital region and lower abdomen. Slowly the feeling of lust and approaching orgasm will build and ultimately result in a unique orgasm that seems to overwhelm in slow motion.

No serious discussion of self-pleasuring touch can avoid mentioning those practices which some men feel are the very dessert of the banquet. First of these: anal stimulation.

Some researchers have suggested that the nerves of the anus and perineum are interconnected with those of the genitals and that the anus is actually an auxiliary sex organ. I would certainly not agree with the second part of that statement and my feeling about the first is this: Virtually every part of the body can be an auxiliary sex organ; our sexuality, our erotic responses are highly individual.

Right now press your fingers firmly into your lower abdomen just above your pubic bone. You'll be applying pressure on your bladder, but you will feel sensations in your penis. Your bladder is therefore a sex organ, right? Unless the term sex organ has no meaning at all, the bladder is not what we would generally think of as a sex organ.

Another example: some men have reported having orgasms through no other stimulation than having their toes sucked. Some unfortunate individuals reach ecstasy by having their buttocks paddled. Women have reported orgasms while having their backs scratched. All of which goes to prove that our entire bodies can be sexually responsive. That's a wonderful thing to realize. But if the language is to have any value we just can't go around talking about knees and elbows as sex organs.

Whether the anus is physiologically invested with particularly erotic sensations is in my opinion highly doubtful. There's no evidence for one thing that we've developed physiological capabilities through evolution that are not necessary to our survival as a species—and there is certainly no survival value in the sexual use of the anus.

From the *psychological* perspective, however, the anus certainly has become eroticized. And if we enjoy playing with our own anuses or having another person play with them as part of our sexual enjoyment, there's nothing demeaning or shameful about understanding why it gives us pleasure.

For one thing there's an actual association between the anus and shame. We've been taught since infancy that it, along with our genital organs, is obscene, smelly, and shameful. For many men shame has become eroticized. That means that some men are turned on sexually by being shamed. That's one form of masochism. Helplessly submitting to anal exposure, fondling, caressing, and penetration, a form of psychological dominance can be highly charged with sexual response. To be sure, that's as true of heterosexual as of gay men.

For others, who have strong urges to express the feminine component of their personalities, the anus obviously becomes a substitute vagina. Wrapping arms and legs around the body of a man, submitting to him passively, is not only erotic (in fact sometimes the erotic aspect is nonexistent) but emotionally fulfilling.

And of course there are men for whom the anal area and the perineum (the area between the anus and the testes) is definitely an erogenous zone. If that's true of you, there s no reason not to enjoy the pleasure which this part of your body offers. However keep your fingernails short and smooth. A tiny hangnail can cause a tear in skin heavily supplied with blood vessels. Even a tiny puncture can lead to profuse bleeding.

Prostate massage. Since this isn't the easiest trick in the world to perform using nothing more than your own body—in this case your fingers—(I'll talk about devices in a later chapter), I won't dwell on the subject here. Suffice it to say that with sufficient massage of the prostate you can trigger ejaculation even without erection or orgasm. And if you're turned on to start with you can achieve the big three—erection, ejaculation, and orgasm—simply by prostate massage without any contact with your penis.

The wisdom of *frequent* prostate massage to ejaculation is another question. We must approach those acts which are not found normally in nature with some prudent questions, not about the *morality* of the acts but about their physiological *wisdom*. Prostate massage is an excellent example of what I mean. That organ's meant to be excited to the point of almost violent spasms through neurochemistry, not manual irritation. Even apart from insults foreign to the natural functioning of the body, the prostate can find all sorts of excuses for swelling and causing the severe discomfort of prostatitis. And of course prostate cancer is the second most common form of that disease in males.

Don't misunderstand: There is no evidence that massaging the prostate either manually or through devices designed for the purpose—or through anal intercourse for that matter—can lead to any ailment or disease. So feel free to make up your own mind about it. But do keep in mind that the opposite has not been proven either. We don't know why some men have severe bouts of prostatitis, why some men develop prostate cancer. What we do know is that, while the penis seems well designed to take a licking and keep on ticking, the prostate is stashed in so intimate and secure a location that only with some devoted effort are we able to make direct contact with it. Since there are so many other fun things we can do with our bodies, personally I'm willing to forego prostate massage.

Auto-fellatio. "It was usually performed while sitting nude on the edge of a bed or chair, for clothing interfered seriously," Dr. Garry Glaye quotes a young patient in *Auto-fellatio & Masturbation*. I would lean my trunk forward as far as possible slide my lower body forward and lock my arms around my upper thighs. By straining forward with the muscles of the neck, thorax, and abdomen while pulling downwards with my arms I was usually able to place my erect penis into my mouth.... This condition also permitted me to penetrate very deeply with my penis and to reach with my lips and tongue my scrotum and even my completely flaccid penis. These practices excited me greatly."

More men than you're likely to imagine have fantasized sucking their own penises. To the man who has a primarily heterosexual orientation, it's the perfect answer. He can satisfy his curiosity about having a penis to suck on while avoiding the humility and shame of admitting that desire to another man. What's more, one isn't really gay or a cocksucker if the only cock one sucks belongs to one's self, right?

Unfortunately for all these curious straights, closet queens, bisexuals and gays, only a very small percentage of the male population has sufficient flexibility and genital endowment to succeed at auto-fellation. Says one man who attempted the act in his mid-20s, "I waited too long. The discs in your spine fuse after a certain age and that's what happened to me. I stretched out on the bed, flipped my feet over my head and walked down the wall, forcing my pelvis closer to my face. But it hurt too much. The idea was sexy as hell, seeing my dick and balls just an inch or two above me, and I did actually shoot in my own mouth and on my face (burns like hell when it gets in your eyes).

"But in all the excitement I ignored the pain in my back and when I was done I thought I was gonna be crippled for life. I'm not kidding you, it took four months for my spine to get back to normal. I thought I'd slipped a disc. You've gotta start practicing sucking yourself off when you're 12 or 14 years old so you can stay flexible. But kids don't think that far ahead when they're that young."

Even the young man quoted by Dr. Glaye had problems at first:

This procedure caused considerable muscular strain, especially at the neck and the sacrum, and often led to considerable discomfort lasting for days after the act. Intestinal pain was sometimes a sequel. But the young man found that by keeping his stomach evacuated he had much more success and less pain in his efforts. He concludes:

> The performance of auto-fellatio was almost always preceded by a period of manual masturbation in which I would bring myself up to a point of orgasm several times. I would do this and then quickly perform auto-fellatio while my erection and arousal were at their most intense level short of ejaculation. Consequently an orgasm followed quickly so that the act itself did not last long. This was in consideration of the muscular difficulties involved. The orgasm was always into the oral cavity and sometimes the ejaculate was swallowed. Sometimes I was able to penetrate my rectum with a finger or grasp my scrotum and these devises were used to increase my ejaculatory ecstasy.
>
> Once I was able to photograph myself in the act of auto-fellatio. This was accomplished with an automatic shutter release on the camera. I kept

these pictures for some time and used them as masturbatory objects.

The young man finally abandoned this unusual form of self-pleasuring because he gained weight around his abdomen and could no longer bend sufficiently.

Let me make it clear here and now that *I do not advocate that you attempt auto-fellatio*. There is a very good reason for that: If by some chance you end up wrecking your back in the effort, I do not wish to be sued for having told you to go ahead and try it. And it certainly is possible to injure yourself, or at least to suffer lingering pain as most of the millions of men who have given this unusual act of solo sex a shot have learned.

But if you choose not to pay attention to this warning (and of course boys will be boys), at least use common sense. Pain is nature's warning. Heed it. Don't get caught in the devil's own trap: Just an inch more and you can put your tongue on it. Go ahead, strain. Ignore the pain. You're so close.

Close indeed—to a trip to a hospital perhaps. And just how are you going to explain to your dear ones why on earth you were forcing your back into such strange positions?

"Masturbation is common in married men and has no particular significance. It is a common misconception that masturbation stops upon marriage and that if it occurs after it the man must be suffering from an emotional disturbance. Neither of these ideas is true."

—Donald W. Hastings, M.D.,
Medical Aspects of Human Sexuality,
December, 1968

Chapter 5
Toys and Other Self-Love Objects

TO THE creative mind virtually everything is a sex fun toy. Any kind of food can be impaled, from the raw liver employed by the teenage star of Philip Roth's *Portnoy's Complaint* to the ducks and geese preferred by the men of Turkey—freshly killed and later eaten.

Says a young man from Pennsylvania who has spent all of his life on a farm, "Watermelons are good. You just cut two cylindrical holes in them, one for your dick and another breather hole so the air can rush in and out of the melon. Sloppy, sure, but great."

"A large green tomato is wonderful," adds the farm youth. So is a dead carp because carp have no teeth. Pumpkins are particularly nice and a large firm one will actually support your weight as you lie upon it and grip it between your thighs."

I have met men who have drilled holes in boards, tables, and piano benches, and had their way with them. Says an outdoorsman "I have been seduced by innumerable crotches of trees."

If there lives a man who hasn't inserted his penis into a cardboard toilet tissue cylinder, he has a creativity quotient of zero. And most of us have tried vacuum cleaner hoses, only to find them hardly worth the trouble. First, the suction is steady rather than pulsing. Second, vacuums are so noisy as to be utterly distracting.

Let's face it: it's the nature of the human male animal to insert his penis into anything that stands still long enough. And if there's nothing nearby to plug, he'll find something to slip over it. Thus, large rings and cylinders are items you don t need to be told about—you've already experimented with them. Those silver key rings, small pieces of stainless steel pipe, large rubber washers, rubber bands (which yank out your pubic hair by the roots), rubber rings cut from bicycle inner tubes, shower curtain rings...I won't discuss these everyday trinkets.

Unfortunately, passion often overrides common sense, and in this chapter we'll be particularly stressing the importance of avoiding that mistake, because the medical literature is replete with examples in which lust to the exclusion of intelligence has led to both embarrassment and injury.

A case in point: While taking a bath, one young man apparently fell in love with the tub faucet and impaled it with his semi-erect penis. He promptly attained a full erection. Apparently the faucet widened an inch or two beyond the opening and his penis swelled into the additional space. Some hours later his mother discovered him still painfully plugged into the faucet. A plumber finally removed the faucet from the wall and he was rushed to the hospital to have the faucet sawed off.

To paraphrase Alexander Pope, "Fools thrust in where wise men..." Edwin W. Hirsch, M.D., gives these case histories in his book *Impotency and Frigidity:*

"I was called to see a man who claimed that his phallus had been accidentally caught in his bedspring. His phallus was tremendously swollen and bluish In color. Cold packs induced a reduction in swelling. priapism gradually diminished.

"Another patient was admitted to the hospital with a large vase lying above his suprapubic region." In other words his penis was trapped in it all the way to his balls. "Patient, while intoxicated, used china vase with small opening in top for masturbatory purposes."

Dr. Hirsch's therapeutic techniques over the years have included withdrawing blood from an organ trapped by a stainless steel ring in order to reduce the organ's size, sawing through a board that strangled another penis, using a grinding wheel to remove a steel nut, resorting to a wire cutter to release a small penis from an emerald ring, and administering antibiotics to clear up an Infection that resulted when one man forced maggots into his urethra.

We will not consider maggots a sex toy. Further, a warning—which I expect you to accept since I am clearly not writing from the perspective of a prude: Nothing—nothing—should ever be inserted in the urethra, the urinary tract of the penis, no matter how much you are tempted to do so. The best you can hope for as a result is an inflamed urethral lining which will cause a deal of discomfort when you urinate, and more discomfort in the form of a maddening itch when it heals. However, the quite likely, and much more serious, aftermath can be infection of the bladder, first evidenced by a blood clot that makes urinating impossible and a visit to the hospital emergency facility necessary. When the blood clot is removed through catheterization (a tube is inserted through the penis into the bladder), profuse bleeding may result. Antibiotics and plenty of water consumption will be prescribed and will probably clear up the infection within three or four days. If not, surgery will be required. And of course, just everybody will find out through the hospital staff or a friend of a friend just why you were hospitalized.

Vibrator cups and sleeves of all sorts are great fun and have little potential for harm other than chafing from overuse. The one exception of course is the 110-volt electrical vibrator when used in a tub full of water. Should you attempt such an experience you won t know whether you're coming or going, although you're likely to be doing both.

The use of electrical devices was actually pioneered by veterinarians trying to breed sexually temperamental animals for money. For example, a bull may not be willing to mount just any old ugly cow simply because the farmer wants him to. The animal's temperamental sexuality threatens to cost the farmer thousands of dollars. The solution—artificial insemination, a process whereby the bull is forced to ejaculate his semen into a container so that the substance later can be carefully implanted into the ugliest cow's uterus.

To this day some farmers still obtain semen by grasping the bull's massive penis with their hands and manually beating the beast off. But that primitive approach is inefficient on large farms—and rumor has it that the wives of some farmers were growing jealous and suspicious. So researchers have developed several more efficient, less dangerous and less time-consuming approaches.

One of the most successful methods now in use is electro-ejaculation. As long ago as 1863, a researcher by the name of Eckhardt produced erections in dogs by passing an electrical current through the area surrounding the sexual organs.

Since then ejaculations have been produced through electrical means without emotional stimulation in rams, bulls, boars, dogs, chinchillas, and foxes. So why not humans? That's what Dr. Robert L. Rowan wondered in 1962. So he tried it on men from whom he needed sperm samples but who were unable to attain erections and therefore could not usually masturbate to ejaculation. That's how Rowan found out something the animals were unable to explain: The electrically stimulated ejaculations were not pleasant. In fact, they hurt like hell. Rowan wrote in the *Journal of Urology*, "It produced so painful a response it was discontinued." Those poor bulls weren't thrashing about in ecstacy but in agony, and voltages low enough to eliminate the pain produced no effect.

But a short while later another doctor, Aquiles J. Sobrero, M.D., described a successful approach in the medical journal *Fertility and Sterility*. In the early 1960's Sobrero made the world's first electronic masturbating machine. He did so to acquire sperm samples from married men suspected of being infertile and incapable of obtaining erections in order to give sperm samples.

It's a gadget you can make yourself at relatively little cost. Sobrero started with an inexpensive Sears vibrator, the type to which you can attach knobs, plastic plates, and such. To the head of the device, Sobrero attached, with adhesive tape, a small collection cup.

Described in technical terms, the cup consists of a 50 milliliter glass crucible. Actually, you and I would call it a whiskey shot glass. A slightly larger plastic funnel—from any local hardware store—is taped into the glass. Sobrero writes, "The cup is applied with gentle pressure to the glans penis and the current turned on. A reflex ejaculation usually occurs between 15 seconds and seven minutes later."

By reflex ejaculation Sobrero means that the man on whom the device is used need not be thinking along sexual lines. In fact he need not even have an erection. Almost before he realizes what's happening he might find himself creaming. We are told that his chances of experiencing the intense orgasmic thrill that usually accompanies ejaculation is only about one in nine but we must remember that this was written almost a quarter of a century ago when even the medical community would have frowned at the thought of a physician deliberately inducing sexual pleasure in another man. In fact, the chances are highly likely that most of these men experienced orgasm.

If you're into spending money, you can find vibrators and pulsaters and massagers in any price bracket you can afford. Some are synthetic vaginas that rapidly vibrate while the inner lining slides back and forth. Others are simple sheathes powered by tiny batteries. They cling to erect penises and vibrate.

The Cadillac of masturbation machines is the Accu-jac. It consists of a plastic sleeve which slides back and forth along the penile shaft as a result of vacuum suction. In the more expensive model, the speed of motion can be controlled from 40 to 100 strokes per minute. Even the stroke length can be varied. What's more, options include an adapter for a companion's simultaneous use and a female adapter, a plastic penis, that will thrust rhythmically into an accommodating orifice.

It's the kind of gadget of which dreams are made—but the price is a nightmare, well up into the $400 range. (The Accu-Jac is appearently no longer made.)

The other devices are available at most of the more sophisticated adult book stores in major cities. They can also be purchased through the mail and many items are advertised in adult sex magazines. If you can't find what you're looking for in heterosexual publications, chalk that up to the nonsensical macho attitude that insists straight men never admit they beat off. Therefore, why would they buy masturbation machines? If you are a straight man and in such a predicament, find a gay friend and ask him for one of his magazines—strictly for the ads of course.

Vacuum Pumps and Enlargers. Among the most popular sex toys is the vacuum penis pump and enlarger. Its attraction is that it swells the cook to dimensions beyond the usual, sometimes beyond our wildest dreams. The sad fact is that virtually none of us is satisfied with the size of our penises. If we stand five inches when erect we want six inches. If we re 10 inches we want 12. And we're absolutely fascinated when, after pumping away for a few minutes on these vacuum contraptions, low and behold we become superdongs. Even after the pump is removed the organ stays engorged for perhaps half an hour to several hours.

There can be great pleasure in sporting a bigger than life phallus, admiring it in the mirror, petting it. The sight and feel of it can have the effect of an aphrodisiac, in fact, and when these pumps are used occasionally and sensibly I'm aware of no cases in which they've caused injury.

But again, as with other sex toys, the potential for abuse exists. The reason the penis enlarges in the first place is that the vacuum forces water from the blood to pass through cell membranes and into the cells themselves, swelling them well beyond their normal size. It doesn't take a genius to realize that, taken to extremes, these cells, the walls of which grow thinner as they expand, have the potential to burst like balloons that are over-inflated. Damaged cells don't function. Too many damaged cells and the organ doesn't function.

What's more, blood vessels, too, can rupture under extreme conditions. A number of men using vacuum pumps to maximum capacity have reported pin-prick leaks of blood through the glans and an entirely purple, bruised-looking shaft. All of this is a result of ruptured capillaries. While I am not personally aware of permanent damage resulting from the use of vacuum pumps, I'd be surprised if some sad idiots haven't suffered hemorrhage and permanent damage to the erectile mechanism because once again lust overwhelmed common sense.

When these pumps were first marketed in the 1960's, physicians gathering at the annual session of the Society for the Scientific Study of Sex stated bluntly, according to Isadore Rubin, Ph.D., writing in *Sexology,* that "This device not only cannot fill the claim of enlarging the penis permanently, but can bring about impotence by damaging the erectile tissue of the penis."

Rubber and Plastic Dolls. These toys started out in England as artificial vaginas equipped with strings so they could be tied to the backs of chairs. Predictably, the Japanese evolved it into a life-sized rubber doll or mannequin originally designed to resemble famous movie stars, with genital areas that were warmed by means of hot water.

Today more sophisticated models include electric motors which move the pelvic area so that the doll can participate in sexual intercourse with its owner.

If you're really into artificial humans, you can buy these dolls with gaping plastic-lined mouths, anuses, vaginas, and male models with erect—even vibrating—penises, vibrating mouths, vibrating everything. In short, if you can imagine it someone has probably built a doll that does it.

I can certainly imagine owning one of these dolls as a novelty, a conversation starter when Aunt Dorothy or the pastor stops by, and even as a sexual experience on those relatively rare occasions when you're in the mood for something really kinky. But it strikes me personally as rather absurd to spend upwards of $100 (for the best models) on a gadget which in all honesty looks and feels like no human being I've ever been to bed with, which is as sexually talented as a log, doesn't appreciate the first thing I might do for it erotically, and stands a good chance of running out of air with my first violent thrust. It is especially absurd in light of the fact that there are so many *real* people who would enjoy having sex with another human being such as myself.

I wonder if men who routinely make love to dolls rather than people aren't relating to the only partner with whom they feel emotionally safe. For any number of reasons they've not come to the point where they can feel sexually confident with another individual, and because our sexuality affects all other aspects of our lives, this is a problem that needs work.

Anal Toys. As I pointed out in a previous chapter, some people—both men and women—experience highly erotic sensations when the anal area is stimulated.

Similarly, we explained that some men are very responsive to nipple stimulation. In both cases the response is highly individualistic; many, perhaps most, men do not find either of these areas sexually responsive. That's fine. Responding or not responding isn't a moral issue. It isn't right or wrong. It simply is; and what non-responders must guard against doing is saying, in effect, "Since I personally don t find that erotic or fun it's wrong to play around with your own asshole."

Such an attitude puts us in the same category as the bigots who feel that solo sex is wrong—or sex apart from marriage, or gay sex, or any activity except that in which the bigots themselves indulge.

In fact, although nature almost certainly didn't intend it as such, the anus has been a de facto sex organ for a very long time. The Mochica Indians of Peru have laws *requiring* anal intercourse between husband and wife from the beginning of her period of lactation following pregnancy until the third year of the offspring's life. This is probably intended to prevent over-population, and couples caught having coitus in the ordinary way during that period were executed. And of course both heterosexual and homosexual men commonly practiced anal sex long before ancient Greece and Rome popularized it.

The working ladies at Parisian houses of prostitution inserted objects into the anuses of their clients during intercourse, reportedly giving great pleasure. In those days apparently "up yours" was not an insult.

One of the most interesting anal devices was used in the Orient and called the anal violin. It consisted of an ivory ball with a length of catgut attached. It was inserted into the anus of the gentleman being pleasured. His partner held the catgut taut and stroked it with the equivalent of a violin bow. That delivered a series of remarkable vibrations to the anal sensory receptors and prostate. As a form of sex play, inserting objects into the anus has a long history.

"I have inserted into my rectum such objects as a length of small rubber hose and a condom. This latter object I attached to a rubber hose so that I could inflate it at will with water or air. I have also derived satisfaction from an ordinary warm-water enema prior to the orgasm." The author of those words is another patient of Dr. Gary Glaye, whom I previously cited. He is by no means unique.

In fact the use of enemas for sexual pleasure is very widespread. It even has a medical name: Klismaphilia. Most doctors don't consider it a dangerous practice as long as the insertion method and substances used in the enema don't damage the intestinal lining and it isn't done so frequently that it drains vital nutrients before the intestines can absorb them .

Probably the most common of all sex toys is the artificial penis used by both men and women. It comes in so many sizes and shapes as well as materials and various degrees of stiffness that the artificial version might well rival even nature's wide assortment. Certainly the double-headed penis does. That's the very favorite sex toy of one young married man whom we'll call John. He says:

"I told my wife before we married that I was probably a latent bisexual, that I enjoyed the passive, masochistic fantasy of having a guy's dick up my ass. She didn't mind. She only asked me to let her try to meet my needs.

"One night she pulled out this monster dong, a three-foot flexible plastic salami with a dick head on each end. She greased the thing up, laid me on my back, lifted up my legs, and before I knew it she had six inches of it up my ass.

"Next thing, she's pushing the other end into her pussy. We moved our bodies together, her legs under mine, embraced, and rocked back and forth in rhythm.

"I got so horny I pulled the thing out of her vagina and slid it into her ass. Then I screwed her. I could feel that big plastic prick right there inside her, separated from my cock by just that thin membrane. God, was it a blast. Enough fantasies to last a lifetime and a half."

Others have made their own artificial penises by melting wax and brushing it on their erect organs layer upon layer until it's a quarter of an inch thick. Depending upon the temperature of the wax, it can be either a painful or stimulating experience—sometimes both. The wax is quickly cooled with cold water and the mold filled with plaster of Paris. Some years ago, a mail order company actually sold a do-it-yourself kit for producing replicas of your own genitals.

A warning, should you decide to make your own plaster penis reproduction: Remove your pubic hair first or the hardened wax might necessitate ripping it out by the roots.

While we're still on the subject of anal toys, I want to present the following stories from the medical literature. You might find some of them humorous, but I hope that you'll also consider them a warning. Engaging in anal sex toy play while your intelligence remains disengaged can lead to injury.

That's what a 42-year-old Puerto Rican man discovered when he shook up a bottle of Coca-Cola and sprayed it up his rectum. Since that didn't prove thrilling enough, he next, according to the physician who treated him later at the hospital, forced the entire bottle into his rectum and could not recover it. Undaunted, he had fashioned a hook from a coat hanger and instructed his wife to use it to remove the bottle. After several unsuccessful attempts, at some time during which he experienced shoulder pain, he came to the hospital.

He arrived at the emergency unit with the coat hanger still protruding from his rectum. Both the bottle and the wire had perforated the intestine and were protruding into his peritoneal cavity—or abdomen. Fortunately, he recovered.

Such stories are not at all rare. An Australian physician describes a patient who inserted a large bottle Of medication into his anus, where it promptly lodged. The patient's explanation was that directions on the bottle had been smeared and he assumed this was as good a method as any for administering the drug.

A Des Moines, Iowa, 24-year-old inserted a large bottle of aftershave lotion, perhaps to reduce the offensive odor of bowel movements. Although surgeons had to dilate the rectum almost to the point of rupture, the bottle was removed without breaking.

Drs. Jay Stuart Haft and H. B. Benjamin of the Medical College of Wisconsin, writing in *Medical Aspects of Human Sexuality,* reported on a virtual cornucopia of objects inserted in the rectums and removed by physicians: A turnip, tooth-brush holder, water tumbler, whiskey bottle, many soft drink bottles, (one persistent individual inserted two at once), a piece of wood, a steer's horn, cucumbers, apples, hard boiled eggs, a condom-covered banana. In each case, emergency medical treatment was required to remove the object.

Saving the lives of some of those sexual experimenters required real creativity on the part of physicians. One man would probably have died from the side effects of a bottle wedged in his intestine if his physician hadn't found a boy with a tiny hand to reach up the man's rectum and remove the object. Another physician removed a glass by filling it with plaster of Paris into which he embedded two strings for extracting the glass. In other cases, the doctors had to perform major surgery opening the abdomen and forcing the objects out of the rectum by manually manipulating the intestine.

Occasionally, objects allowed to remain in the intestine migrate through the intestinal wall and into other parts of the body. One man was found with several sharp objects lodged in his buttocks.

Without exception these injuries result from allowing lust to override common sense. For example, a soft drink bottle with a relatively small opening might slide into the anus without great difficulty. However, the wide, flat bottom will lodge itself against the rectal sphincter when removal is attempted. Without specialized medical equipment, such as the forceps used to deliver babies, and the help of someone knowledgeable of the workings of the rectal sphincter, it will be all but impossible to remove the bottle. That fact is obvious to anyone who gives it some thought—but some men, swept up in sexual excitement, turn off their common sense.

Obviously, a drinking glass poses an even greater problem, since the rim will wedge itself around the ring-like sphincter. In some cases, glasses have broken in the attempt to remove them, slashing surrounding flesh and leading to hemorrhage.

Fetishes. Society currently holds in some distain those whose libidos are stimulated by various objects that have no sexual interest to the majority. Perhaps the most common fetish is women's underwear. Some men achieve erection and even ejaculation with orgasm simply by handling bras and panties. Others respond to high-heeled shoes or garments made of rubber or leather.

Apart from the psychological implications—and I'm not sure there are any worth being concerned about—the fact is that *most* men are fetishists, at least in the broad sense. The sight of a naked female breast will drive some men in Western society into a frenzy, while on some Pacific islands and in much of Africa the bare buttocks of the female will do the same. In such places, breasts have no erotic value whatever. My opinion is that as long as fetishes do not interfere with normal sexuality—that is as long as one can enjoy sex apart from the fetish—the fetish object is nothing more than a sex toy.

Lester Dearborn, former director of the Marriage Counseling Service of Boston, reports on a man who could make love only when the woman agreed to wear a rubber bathing cap. After his marriage, his wife agreed to meet that small need of her husband's, especially since he was an excellent lover who satisfied her thoroughly. However, she consulted Dr. Dearborn to find out just how abnormal the practice was. Even in this case, where the fetish was necessary to sexual function, Dr. Dearborn assured the woman that there was nothing wrong with use of the cap. He also talked to the man, to put his mind at ease.

That small bit of reassurance, incidentally, had a dramatic effect on the man, who had always harbored some guilt about this abnormality. As a result, he became much more self-confident at work, and that led to a series of promotions.

To summarize: sex toys can add variety and freshness to solo sex sessions and, although you may think you are the only one in the world who has inserted his penis into that particular bizarre orifice, whatever it might be, the odds are outstanding that you aren't. Until you've tried to make love to a jarful of fruit flies, a vice, a power sander, the bilge pump of a boat, a hole in the mud, and hundreds more objects, these being merely those that have come to my personal attention, you can be assured that you're not unique, only one of millions of creative, imaginative men who are sexually normal and active in the world today.

Enjoy—but remember that goal number one isn't to attain pleasure. It's to keep all the equipment intact for another day.

Chapter 6
Sex Secrets and Solo Sex

"**I WAS** on the Tappan Zee Bridge, over the Hudson, heading for New York. It was three in the morning and there wasn't another car in sight anywhere, so I decided to open it up, see just how fast the old Chrysler would go. I hit 110 and the pedal wasn't even to the floor yet, and then I thought, with that rail flashing by and the water down there, a blowout in that bald front tire and I'm dead."

Allen was on his way back to college in Westchester after a two-day sexual marathon with his girl in Scranton, Pennsylvania. Sex was the furthest thing from his mind. Yet, the thought of crashing through the guard rail and plummeting to the icy water below gave him a furious erection. In just a few seconds of manipulation he reached orgasm.

Danger, Allen had discovered, is an aphrodisiac.

Allen doesn't talk about this secret sex kick of his to many people because, as he says, "I'm sort of ashamed of it. I mean, it really is kinky, isn't it, getting off like that? Some people might even think I'm nuts jerking off at 110 miles an hour."

That's one of the things secret sex kicks have in common—they're not the sort of thing we'd discuss over Thanksgiving dinner with the relatives. We don't consider them typical. We might even feel that they're abnormal, deviant. But we're mistaken if we hold that belief.

As we'll discover in this chapter and the three to follow, some of our secret sexual kicks are virtually universal. A few might even be intrinsic to normal sexual response.

A second reason we rarely discuss these secret sexual pleasures is that when acted out without restraint they're often illegal. In Allen's case the speed limit on the Tappan Zee Bridge is 55 miles and hour, which he succeeded in doubling.

Perhaps the most common secret sex kick is exhibitionism. When practiced under certain circum-stances, it's considered a deviation and a crime which can lead to imprisonment. Obviously the circumstances make all the difference in the world. If you exhibit your body on a stage before adults paying to view it in order to be erotically stimulated, you're likely to be considered a performer and be well paid. However, should you be discovered skinny-dipping on a desolate, lonely beach, with no desire to be seen much less to arouse sexual desire, you're a prime candidate for charges of indecent exposure or sexual exhibitionism.

Finally, secret sex kicks usually involve danger. Not necessarily as blatant a danger as in Allen's case, or the legal danger of the exhibitionist. Perhaps it's only the symbolic danger of being bound and gagged by a playmate, or having sex with a dominant stranger. Whether the danger is real or symbolic, it is usually present to some degree in our most secret sexual practices.

In the next few chapters we're going to learn how to use our secret sex kicks to enhance our solo sex pleasure. I'll show that these pleasures at their core are not in the least deviant, but merely expressions of the emotional needs of various personalities.

And perhaps most importantly, I'll show how these needs can be met in ways that offend no one and therefore break no laws. I am specifically *not* encouraging the breaking of laws. I believe that complete sexual pleasure can be experienced while obeying the laws, puritanical, thoughtless, and juvenile though they often are. That is what I urge. Think of it this way if you like: Rather than discovering greater pleasures, you can find your solo sex life seriously disrupted if you get arrested for breaking the law.

Let's begin with the matter of danger. Few people are sufficiently tuned in to their sexual feelings to realize how closely libido—or sexual desire, lust— and fear are related in the human psyche. Yet, the evidence is irrefutable. On the most basic level, *sexual response, aggression and fear are triggered in the very same small area of the hypothalamus,* a part of the brain that controls emotion. Beyond that, there is the testimony that many people give without realizing exactly what they're saying. For example:

"I can't get enough of Freddie or Friday the 13th or any of them horror films," says one boy in his late teens. "They scare the shit out of me. I practically cream in my pants."

"Some men just look--well, dangerous," says 18-year-old Ellie, a Tampa, Florida, waitress. "There's something in their eyes. They look a little crazy and rough like they could hurt you. I see them all the time in this place [the diner where she works]. Some of them ask me out. I always say no, but the thought of being alone with them in the woods at night is enough to get me off."

Says psychoanalyst Robert Stoller, M.D., professor of psychiatry at UCLA's School of Medicine, "Orgasm is not merely discharge or ejaculation but a joyous, mega-lomaniac burst of freedom from anxiety (analogous to the release of great laughter following a beautifully executed joke...)" He adds, "we move between the sense of danger and the expectation of escape from danger to sexual gratification."

Danger actually intensifies our sexual desire and in-creases the thrill of the orgasm. To seek risks and dan-ger—symbolic or real—as part of sexual expression is often healthy and normal. Most of us begin to equate sex with danger even before adolescence. We played doctor with the girl (or boy) next door knowing that all hell would break loose if we were discovered. The game was deli-ciously exciting, all the more so, because it was forbidden and dangerous.

So it continues through the early teenage years: Seeking out Dad's pornographic magazines in spite of the potential for punishment; early experiments with solitary sex, the pleasure more intense because of its "sinfulness," our helplessness against the temptation of "evil," the inevitability of our yielding to our "depraved," orgasms.

(Perhaps instead of condemning the puritans of the world for their mindless attacks on sexual pleasure, we should express gratitude to them for making "sex" evil and dangerous, thereby substantially increasing the joy of sex for humankind.)

Socially and religiously disapproved sexual acts are far and away the most common risks. One example is oral sex. "The main reason I like '69' so much," says one young man, "is that it's so dirty. I mean, the *idea* of it. My mom was always saying, 'Watch what you put in your mouth,' and at the same time, 'Don't play with your pee pee, those dirty parts.' So what can be more dirty and sexy than having somebody suck my cock while I do them?"

For some, masturbation is infused with sin and risk. For others, mixed race romance is dangerous. Still others find the added thrill in fetishes or by cross-dressing. The goal is always the same—to create a sense of danger because it intensifies the feeling of lust.

Says Dr. Stoller, "An awareness that one is sinning often increases sexual excitement."

Another common sexual danger—much more so than most people would guess—is the controlled exhibitionism I mentioned earlier. That's because exhibitionism is direct and to the point. One needn't have a master's degree to recognize the sexual power of an erect penis.

In fact, says Reinhart Quinsel in his book *Sexual Exhibitionism,* We all have an exhibitionist in us struggling to come out. Most of us manage for this reason or that to control the impulse or contain it or simply to let it die for lack of opportunity or fear of social disapproval.

In the next chapter I'll show how many men enjoy a sense of danger and power, yet remain within the letter of the law by practicing a safe, symbolic exhibitionism that offends no one, keeps these men out of trouble, and gives them all the pleasure they seek.

Often the search for danger leads to other types of illegal acts. A New York City stockbroker, now in his late 20's, says, "From the time I was 18 or 19, I had this compulsion to screw young girls—14, 15, 16. It wasn't that I found them sexier, but that's what I thought at the time. Fact is, some of them were dogs. It was the idea that it was so *wrong*, so *dangerous*, that made it so hot for me.

Fortunately this fellow fell in love with one 16-year-old, dated her exclusively for three years and married her. In his fantasies she remains his underaged sex partner.

For a relatively few men, actual rape is the secret sex kick. (Rape *fantasies,* on the other hand, are extremely common among both men and women, as you'll see later.) Here, too, the act of rape is fraught with danger, but not the danger you might think at first. The exhibitionist gets his thrill at the thought of being observed, but the rapist doesn't find pleasure in the idea that he might be caught. Far from it. Being caught is the furthest thing from his mind. And this is a point that has been almost completely overlooked: The rapist gets his pleasure in a cowardly fashion. He doesn't even have the courage of your every-day exhibitionist. He gets his excitement by *identifying with the woman victim.* By terrorizing her and sharing that terror he feels both danger and power, the masculine dominance that otherwise eludes him.

Evidence gathered in an exhaustive study by Dr. Menacham Amir, an Israeli criminologist, supports that statement. In 37 percent of all rapes, says Amir, the rapist either brandishes a weapon or threatens his victim with death, whether or not either is necessary. In 45 percent of the cases the rapist beats his victim, and chokes her in 12 percent. The violence is needed not to subdue the victim but because, unwilling to confront sexual danger himself, the rapist gets his kicks secondhand through the woman.

If actual rape happens to be your secret sex kick, you must weigh seriously what this says about your own masculine identity. I'm certainly not going to preach to you—that's not what this book is about. But the unequivocal fact is that you need as much help as you can get to realign your sexual personality. That isn't impossible, as much as it may seem so to you now. Talk to a psychiatrist who isn't a prude. Tell him you want him to help you find other safer, healthier ways to experience danger in sex. If he doesn't know what you're talking about, give him a copy of this book to read.

Another extreme form of erotic danger might be called the James Bond Syndrome—the need to confront physical danger in order to become sexually aroused. The inimitable 007 seems utterly incapable of lovemaking unless he and his partner are within microseconds of annihilation. That awareness alone seems to get his juices flowing.

Western society isn't alone in recognizing the sex/violence link. The people of Tahiti still honor an ancient myth, the story of Lakat, a beautiful girl who remained a virgin long after her playmates had become mothers. When Ro-mi, a young man of the village, befriended her, she confessed, "I do not want to make love. I want to go shark riding."

Ro-mi warned her of the extreme danger, but in his heart he understood this strange passion. He agreed to help Lakat, and the next day he paddled her in his canoe to shark-infested waters, found a relatively small shark and maneuvered beside it.

In an instant Lakat leaped upon the fish and twined her long legs around it. Ro-mi was stunned by the beauty of her naked body clutching the shark, her breasts pressed against its rough back. Suddenly he felt an overwhelming fear and surge of desire.

Lakat felt the same. She plunged her knife deep into the shark's underbelly and a wonderful orgasmic sensation swept through her.

Back in the canoe, Lakat lay on her back before Romi. She pulled him to her and there in the warm sun, lost her virginity.

Men have experienced erection—and a few men have reported orgasms—on roller coasters, while skydiving, skiing rapidly, tobogganing, galloping a horse at breakneck speed. The great psychoanalyst Theodore Reik has reported that soldiers, before entering a particularly dangerous battle, have masturbated as many as ten times. Men and women trapped in burning buildings have spent their last moments in sexual embrace.

Why? Why is there the "heightened excitement" that Dr. Robert Stoller has observed "in performing a sexual act where they [the participants] might be caught" breaking a custom or taboo or statute? "This is conscious risk-taking and is used to add sauce to the dish."

That "sauce" is also the reason that some men risk long prison terms or death; sex without danger holds no excitement for them.

Writing in the *Journal of Sex Research*, psychotherapist John C. Sonne suggests that sex alone has the power to triumph over death, which is what danger ultimately symbolizes. "Sexual intercourse experienced by the most fully developed human is a re-enactment of almost complete dissolution," he says. We actually forsake our consciousness—our personal existence—in the sex act, but through the orgasm we not only live, but live in ecstasy.

"Sexuality," says Alexander Lowen, M.D., of the institute for Bio-Energy Analysis, "is the expression of life and the antithesis of death."

So intrinsic to our sexual natures is the need for danger that Rolf Milonas, in his *Fantasex,* a book of erotic games, offers many fantasies that are infused with social, legal or life-threatening dangers. Among them:

* His partner has switched places with a 16-year-old virgin.

* Their old-fashioned father keeps her from dating, but doesn't suspect her brother, who is consoling her in her room.

* The audience will demand their cruel punishment unless pleased and excited by their performance on the lighted stage.

* On her honeymoon cruise, while her husband is playing Monopoly, a dark stranger invites her to his cabin. She goes.

* If he doesn't perform properly they will make him a eunuch.

* She risks her life to be with him.

* He takes her to a friend's house and forces her to service the friend.

* She has betrayed him and knows that they will kill him as he leaves the house.

Many couples have invented their own symbolic dangers, thereby lifting their sex lives to greater pleasures than they had ever imagined. The key is to keep the risks symbolic—controlled make-believe. Always keep one ear tuned to the real world.

Obviously the safest—and sometimes the only—way to enjoy some bizarre solo sex games without risking unpleasant consequences, is through pure fantasy, and we'll have a great deal to say about that later. By pure fantasy, we mean, that which takes place entirely in the imagination, without props of any sort, and although some people are quite well versed in this area, for others it comes less easily.   Nonetheless, those who have developed it to its fullest know that sexual fantasies can be more real, more intense than reality itself, and that is why we will discuss it in Part III, *The Ultimate Orgasm and the Brain*.

In symbolic acting out of sexual secrets, you'll find that you can blend reality with fantasy for very satisfying solo sex. Many men do this regularly without ever giving it a thought.   For example, one man reports masturbating while leaning out of a window naked, although only the upper half of his body is visible.

Another squeezes his testicles harshly while bringing himself to orgasm, pretending that he is about to be mutilated. As you'll see, such solo sex games are not at all unusual, and like solo sex itself, nothing can be gained by a society-wide ostrich-like approach to such phenomena: A denial that these practices both exist and exist commonly. Such denial creates an inescapable circular problem. We deny because we fear, we fear because we do not understand. We do not understand because we deny. The more productive approach is to recognize forthrightly what goes on sexually in our society, to examine that behavior objectively, to deal forcefully with that which is harmful, such as rape and sexual coercion, and to keep our noses out of the rest. In the next few chapters, I'll discuss the most common secret sex acts and show how some men have used them to enhance the pleasure of solo sex.

THE JOY OF SOLO SEX

"Sex is a path to liberation.
Sex is a path to enlightenment.
Sex is a path to the King/Queendom of God/dess.
Sex is not the only path.
Not the best path for all of us
but definitely a powerful path."

—*Sacred Orgasms*, Kenneth Ray Stubbs

Chapter 7
Simulated Exhibitionism

EXHIBITIONISM IS the most common of all prosecuted sexual offenses. During a period of only a few months recently, I came across these newspaper accounts of men who had been arrested for this activity:

Stroudsburg, Pennsylvania, Gateway to the Poconos: A young man decided that the open spaces and rolling hills were an ideal setting for a naked stroll in the sun. He made two miscalculations, however. First, he chose a day in January, during subfreezing temperatures and an ice storm, his only protection being a pair of nylons. Second, being the only one wandering through the fields in such weather, he was easily observed and arrested.

A few months later a 21-year-old Fort Lauderdale man, frustrated with rush-hour traffic that ignored his attempts to hitchhike, stripped naked to catch attention— and hopefuily a ride. He got one, to the local jail where he was charged with hitchhiking and creating a diversion.

Jose Gonzales, practically overcome by Venezuelan temperatures of 104°F in the shade, was arrested for walking naked along the street. His reasonable response: "What do you want me to do, die of the heat?"

THE JOY OF SOLO SEX

From Chicago, Mike Royko reported on the notorious jogger who always wore a flashy sweatshirt, running shoes, and dark shorts with a white stripe at the hips. He was arrested when an observant police officer noticed that those flashy shorts were actually "flashing"—the stripes were merely painted on the man's skin.

At Purdue University in Indiana, 59 students were placed on disciplinary probation and eight others received probated suspension when they held a public nude Olympics, just as the ancient Greeks did.

These are just a few of the thousands of cases of exhibitionism reported in local papers in the past few years. Taken as a whole, they suggest some thought-provoking points:

* The majority of exhibitionists don't exhibit erections. Take, for example, the Gettysburg man arrested for driving naked through the Lehigh Valley Mall parking lot. The two victims who saw him, both women in their 20's, specifically didn't see him display an erection. The man explained that he had been taking a nap in his car and felt more comfortable undressed. He simply forgot to put his clothes back on. Quite an unlikely story, but the probable truth that he simply felt like being naked obviously would have been a hopeless defense in these days of body-negativism.

* Another man, this one from Illinois, also found driving naked on a hot summer day, insisted that his air-conditioner had broken and he would have died from the heat had he remained dressed.

* On those occasions when an investigation is conducted into the psychological status of the exhibitionist, he is almost invariably found to be under great emotional stress at work, at home, or both. The act of exhibitionism is a temporarily successful means of

relieving that stress. It is a gesture which, in effect, says to those who impose burdensome and senseless rules, "Fuck off."

* Exhibitionists are almost invariably men.

Less than one percent of exhibitionists are female, perhaps because conventional society permits women to display much of their bodies without giving offense, writes John P. Callan, M.D., in *The Journal of the American Medical Association.*

However those of us who are in touch with our own thoughts and fantasies realize that exhibitionism can be just what it seems—an act of sexual pleasure. Exhibitionism, or showing off the merchandise, is normal throughout the animal world, presumably including that of the human animal. Even today, many primitive tribes have orgiastic fertility dances in which males flash females and vice versa. The men are stimulated sexually both by seeing female sex parts, and also by being seen in lusty arousal.

We of the civilized genre no doubt have the same instincts as our primitive brethren, a strutting pheasant, posturing monkeys, and mane-tossing stallions. Although what is natural is not always legal, we can't help responding intensely to behavior that's been an intrinsic part of the sex act for millions of years—so the argument goes. For some men, doing their thing before an audience is definitely the greatest sexual high. For them, "display" behavior lifts them to the highest sexual intensity they have ever experienced:

"This [getting naked] began in the form of masturbatory orgies in a woodod area.... I also drove a car while nude and derived great pleasure from the orgasm which resulted. Subsequently, I practiced this form of masturbation until thoroughly aroused and then would step out of the car on some lonely road and ejaculate."

Dr. Garry Glaye quotes this young man in his book *Auto-fellatio and Masturbation:* "At home I duplicated these practices by nocturnal wanderings. Once or twice I hung the lower part of my nude body out of a window and ejaculated. Another time I climbed out on the roof of a porch in the dead of night to perform nude masturbation. And I frequently wandered nude around the backyard, ultimately having an orgasm there."

Note that none of these acts is likely to be observed by another person, especially if performed at night or with great care. For example, it isn't difficult to find privacy in the woods and to hear someone approachlng from a great distance. What goes on inside an automobile can be observed only by those passing in large trucks or buses, and at nlght it's possible to see the headlights of approaching cars long before the cars themselves are visible on lonely roads. The man who tells these stories was never arrested for such acts.

Others push the limits even farthur. (I must specify that I am neither proposing nor condoning but merely reporting these acts. To do otherwise could be interpreted as inciting to commit a crime which of course I would not dream of doing.)

"I started masturbating in pubic toilets without bolting the door," says one young man cited by Quinsel, "half hoping, half fearful that someone would interrupt me and see my erect organ in my hand."

"My girl and I go to a public park late at night—it's safe in our town," says another man. "After midnight the streets are empty. We strip right down to the skin when the weather's warm and screw on the grass in front of the bushes. We realize that if a car came around the corner we might be seen, but none ever has so far. It's the *possibility* that makes it so exciting. But if it ever really happened, we'd probably drop dead of shock."

A man who lives in a suburban Boston development says, 'We screw by the window a lot, but the room's dark inside and with the street lights shining on the glass, nobody can see a thing—unless we open the window, which we do sometimes just for the hell of it."

Some men move even closer to the fine line between simulated and actual risk-taking. Quinsel gives this example:

"...She went to the toilet. I made some excuse [to her husband] to get out into the hallway and listen outside the bathroom door. I got my penis out and started masturbating leaning against the wall and holding my handkerchief ready to catch the sperm. The bathroom door opened and Laura came out. I didn't stop, I just stood there doing it, looking at her the whole time. She went very white. Her eyes were on fire. She came and stood so close I could smell her perfume. She was breathing heavily."

He climaxed. Afterward both returned to the room without saying a word, but that moment of exquisite danger ultimately cost the young man who experienced it a long and valuable friendship when the wife told her husband about it to make him more attentive.

A middle-aged man now living near Philadelphia submits this list of dubious achievements:

"I have stuck my dick out of hotel room windows and shot my juice to the sidewalks below in Tampa, Dallas,

THE JOY OF SOLO SEX

Houston, San Francisco, Ontario, Quebec, New York, Chicago, Philadelphia, Baltimore, Washington, Venice, Rome, various cities in Mexico, Hawaii, and Australia.

"I have dumped my load in airplanes at 31,000 feet, trains speeding from Philadelphia to Chicago, in cars and buses. I've stripped totally naked in the back seat of a crowded bus for the purpose of solo sex and jerked off in an airplane when the seats in front of me and behind me were occupied. In a convertible that I was driving. I stripped nude, drove alongside a truck and jerked off knowing the truck driver was watching me. Tooting his horn, he signaled that he was masturbating too.

"I once turned the light on in my room and stood naked at the window of the West Side YMCA in Manhattan and beat off out the open window while another man on the far side of the horseshoe-shaped building did the same across the courtyard.

"And I haven't written even half of the wild things I've pulled off!"

The man who wrote the above insists that he has been carrying on these adventures for almost a quarter of a century without being observed, much less arrested, with the exception of the mutually shared YMCA and truck driver incidents. The key, he says, is that "I never lose my cool. Part of my mind is always alert to the dangers. Even in the back of the bus, when I was naked, the other passengers were all up front. I had my jogging shorts around my ankles and my T-shirt up around my neck. I could have gotten back in shape in half the time it would have taken anyone to get back to where I was sitting."

Still, some of these more outlandish acts are very risky and I am compelled to discourage taking such chances. They're simply not necessary.

We've already discussed the most common example of symbolic exhibitionism: the use of mirrors. Raymond B. has been using mirrors to enhance solo sex since his mid-teens—for more than 20 years. He's a connoisseur of mirror sex, claims to be the world's only expert on the subject and has impressive photographs to prove it.

"It's one thing to jerk off in front of a mirror," he says, "and another to see yourself from perspectives most people can't even imagine." Among some of Raymond's exhibitionist achievements:

—Kneeling on a table, a mirror on a chair behind reflecting into another mirror in front of him, so that he can look forward and see his genitals dangling and anus helplessly exposed.

—A board between two chairs, a large hole drilled in the center of it, through which his penis is inserted. Mirrors beneath and to the side reflect only the disembodied phallus thrusting in and out of the board and ejaculating.

—Large mirror permanently installed above bed.

—Entire walls and ceiling area of bath and shower mirrored.

What might ordinarily seem to be an obsessional need to see his own reflection doesn't appear to be a problem in Raymond B.'s case. "I use mirrors with sex whenever I do it by myself," he says. "It's like watching somebody else, and at the same time knowing somebody's watching me. But when I'm with another person, we don't use mirrors. Well, of course they get a kick out of the bath, and the one over the bed, but there's nothing compulsive about them.

Some men actually sublimate the exhibitionistic instinct by unabashedly stroking themselves in front of strange women—who appear on television.

One of the most common methods of solo exhibitionism is the taking of self-portraits. Millions of men have prized collections of photos depicting themselves in various solo sex acts which they've taken using timers, mirrors, or for extreme close-ups, special lenses.

Shared Exhibitionism

The nice thing about having a friend who is also into exhibitionism is that you can both be true voyeurs as well as exhibitionists and still maintain the sexual independence that sometimes makes solo sex preferable. Often during adolescence, we spontaneously play these "look at me" games without giving them much thought. One young man told Dr. Quinsel:

"We would pull all the curtains in his mother's bedroom and then both of us would undress and Daniel, that was my friend's name, would pose like a discus thrower and I would pose like a runner or a Greek god. Something of that nature. We didn't touch each other much. We enjoyed showing off our bodies, I guess."

Very often, the showing off is more genitally oriented, and frequently it does lead to contact and even mutual masturbation:

"I think I was 15. There were only three other boys in the neighborhood, and they were all 13, so I had a two-year headstart on them. We formed a club, which met in the basement of my house. We had some chairs and tables there, and a bathroom.

"One day we got to talking about cocks, and I said I had a big one. All three of them wanted to see it, so I stripped and laid nude across the table. Don't ask me why I did that. I mean, why I stripped in the first place, instead of just pulling it out and showing it to them. Instead, I stripped completely, even my shoes and socks, and then, to give them the best possible view, so they'd see my balls, my pubic hair, my asshole, any part of me they wanted to see, I laid up there on the table.

"Well, you know that turned me on like hell. Here they are, these three innocent kids, one on each side of me, the other between my legs, their eyes wide and bulging like hard-boiled eggs, just staring at my cock. I mean, they were *in awe* of it!

"One of them says, 'Damn, that's the biggest cock in the world!' He actually asks if he can feel it, and of course I say okay. Another says, 'You got giant balls,' so I tell him he can play with them if he wants.

"The third guy's quiet, but he's practically salivating, he's so turned on by my dick. All their faces are red with excitement, but this third kid's actually panting. He pulls his eyes off my cock for a second, looks up at my face. I smile, encouraging him, and he finally says, 'I want to make it shoot.'"

The boy on the table granted permission to the younger friend, and spread his legs wide. "He just moved between my legs and took my cock in one of his hands, my balls in the other, and started moving it up and down, nice and slow. I stretched out, arched my pelvis upward, watching the other guys watch me. It was a thrill to beat all thrills, I'm telling you. The power of knowing that I was driving them crazy. I must have shot three feet over my head. The dumb thing is, although they asked to do it again, I never agreed. I just felt it was wrong."

It's possible that the guilt resulted from having crossed the line between a solo sex act enhanced by mutual exhibitionism to frankly homosexual behavior, which is particularly condemned among teenage boys.

For many men, sexually explicit letter writing and receiving is a highly stimulating exhibitionistic activity that still maintains the advantages of solo sex. If your only response to writing anything is that it's the same misery as your high school English class assignments, you should know that there are literally thousands of erotically oriented correspondence clubs in the United States alone.

Most members use post office boxes for a smart reason: They want to be certain that they maintain a certain distance between themselves and the people to whom they write. Certainly some letter writers use the clubs to meet face to face with people who share their interests, but much more often the clubs are a safe and apparently legal safety valve for exhibitionism and voyeurism. (I say apparently because it will take a far wiser pereon than I to keep abreast of what is legal from one day to the next in each of the 50 states.)

A word to the wise: If you want to maintain complete control over whether or not your pen pal shows up unexpectedly on your doorstep one morning, be sure to use a post office box. Never send money to your correspondent for any reason, no matter how plausible or pathetic the situation. And very important: Never buy or exchange photos of naked people *if any of them are under the age of 18.*

Don't put anything in writing that you could be blackmailed for.

If this seems a rather severe approach to having a special pen pal, keep the following in mind: While some pen pal clubs are composed entirely of legitimate seekers like you and me, in others 50 percent and more of those placing ads are running a hustling operation of one sort or another. They include male and female prostitutes, con artists out to win your trust and then to give you a sob story, a business scheme, and offer to sell you precisely the sort of pornography that you have indicated drives you the wildest, or to execute some other means of separating you from your money.

There are also blackmailers on the other end of that postal highway.

And there are also *postal inspectors who have in the past frequently advertised and delivered kiddie porn, then arrested the buyers, somehow ignoring the fact that they, as peddlers, ought also to have been prosecuted.*

Don't misunderstand. Kiddie porn should be stopped, and it has been, to all intents, at least as a commercial venture in the United States. I strongly discourage even sexual fantasies involving children, because I believe there is truth to the Biblical proposition, "As a man thinketh in his heart, so is he." I believe that dwelling on the pleasure of such acts as one's only sexual expression hinders the normal process of sexual maturation.

But I also adhere to another Biblical passage: "Shall we do evil that good may abound? God forbid!" To break the law in order to uphold it is fascism. It is totalitarianism. And the government of a free democracy would never be able to get away with such behavior except that it now uses the excuse of prosecuting child molesters. I propose that even the need to apprehend the purchasers of kiddie porn is not a worthy altar on which to slaughter the freedoms for which this nation exists. There are other ways to get the job done.

Yet, it is happening. Be careful.

Then there is telephone sex. In an effort to explore this—and also computer clubs—as an avenue of solo sex exhibitionism, I did some in-depth research a while back. Here are my experiences and findings:

A sensual recorded female voice answers the phone, reminds us that we will he paying through the nose for this service, and that a chime will sound every five minutes to remind us of our pending bankruptcy. She warns that the party line is for adults only and promises us a good time.

"Hello," says the sexy live voice. "Hello, is anybody out there?" Silence.

"Hello, somebody. Is anybody listening?"

She's the hostess, paid to keep the conversation flowing. We're not supposed to know that, we're supposed to think she's just an ordinary woman out to have some fun.

"Come on, guys, speak up."

I don't want to speak up, I want to listen. It's my quarter, and I'll do what I want.

Actually, it's a lot more than a quarter. It's from 55 cents to more than a dollar per minute, depending upon the particular party line dialed. The amount can soar very quickly. A teenager in Albuquerque, New Mexico, ran up a bill of $8,000 before Daddy discovered how junior was getting his kicks.

In fact, many companies running the "gab lines," as they're called, have taken steps to avoid the complete economic ruin of their clientele. When the billng to a single telephone number reaches more than $300 in a single week on an adult line, additional calls are electronically barred. Which means that you can't blow more than $1,200 on any one party line in a single month.

It's obvious how useful that credit blocking is. Washington, D.C., has 12 lines, Chicago 40, New York and San Francisco about 50 each and Pennsylvania leads the nation with 82. Theoretically, you could call each of them, remain well under the $300 weekly ceiling and blow $280,000 monthly—plus tolls.

Male: "Between 7:30 and nine is good for me."
Female: "Okay. You mean tomorrow?"
Male: "Yeah, I get home around 5:30. I eat. I like to rest awhile after supper. Anything's going on I get washed. So about 7:30. Got to get going now. I get up early."
Female: "Okay, then. All right, bye bye. (Silence.) Hello, out there. Hello, somebody. Is anybody out there?"

Indeed, someone is out there. According to Media 4, one of the largest party line sponsors in the U.S., approximately 700,000 use the service every week in the New York area alone. Brendan Corrigan of Caliber Commications, a competitor with operations in New York and Philadelphia, reports about 100,000 callers a day.

Why? Why pay good money to talk to strangers with whom you have nothing in common about things that sometimes bore you silly?

"Yeah, sure it's sometimes like that," says Bob, a young salesman in Philadelphia. "But the party lines all have their own personalities. Some you like, some you don't. You stick with the ones with your kind of people."

If you're interested in finding the lines most likely to enhance your solo sex life, you need to do some careful investigating. Otherwise you could spend a lot of money before you find out that you've tuned in to a line for t.v. soap fans, for example. As *Newsweek* pointed out recently, "There are lines for blacks, gays, soap and trivia fans—and of course those totally awesome and tireless talkers: teenagers."

First, there are chit-chat lines for the lonely. For the most part, the conversation is polite, if chaotic. Up to ten people can be on a single line at once. They paid their money. If they all want to talk simultaneously, who's to stop them?

But sometimes people do prefer to listen. In a telephone version of *West Side Story*, two people step out of the crowd and begin communicating. They find they have interests in common, and the hostess, acting as matchmaker, might be able to switch them to a private connection. More often, she'll try to keep other talkers silent long enough for the two to exchange their own phone numbers.

Woman: "Will you be quiet a minute? This is business. I need to get his number."

Hostess: "Okay. What's his name?"

Woman: "Andre."

Hostess: "Andre, are you listening?"

Andre: "Yeah."

Hostess: "Give your number."

Andre: (Gives number.)

Hostess: "Okay." (Andre and woman hang up.)

Man: "Anybody want to give me their number?"

But the main subject of the party line agenda, you'll be happy to know, is sex. The companies know it. So does the Federal Communications Commission. So do the right-wing preachers. (Doesn't anybody ever wonder just how these guys know so *much* about the evils of society?)

The state regulatory agencies also know, which is why Pennsylvania now relegates party lines to a 556 exchange and all would-be callers must first obtain an application form from their telephone companies before they're able to connect to that exchange. Most other states have similar regulations or are developing them. The federal government, too, is expected to get into the act, ostensibly in order to prevent those under 18 from making such calls.

(There is Something magical about the 18th birthday. The day before it arrives we are innocent and virginal, blessedly free from the need for sexual gratification. The next morning, we awaken mature sexual beings full of lust and legally permitted sex with anyone except those a day or more younger than we are.)

Some lines claim to have "bouncers" who cut in when a particular caller becomes obscene. First the bouncer warns, then he disconnects. But few callers have ever heard the bouncer's voice, and the consensus is that obscenity is determined within the context of the conversation. When the group is talking about the weather and some clown begins to describe his current relationship with his genitals, that's obscene; when everyone is talking about their genitals, that's fun—and profitable for the company.

Man: "So what are you doing?"

Woman: (Breathing heavily.) "Playing with myself."
Man: "Feel good?"
Woman: "You bet. Oh, I'm wet. But I'd like to be playing with your balls, too."
Man: "What would you do with them?"

Especially late at night, that's the way it goes. On occasion, three, four or more chime in at once.

"Hey, what about me? I got balls, too."

"I can take care of you, big boy." (A high, sweet voice, but definitely male.)

"Get off the line, fag."

"Let him talk. Maybe you'll learn something."

"Hey, woman, you ever try it the Greek way?"

"That's what I had in mind," says the gay boy.

That's where the really big money is in party lines, a kind of group dial-a-porn with the hostess filing in the dull spots with lurid descriptions of her current state of nakedness and self-stimulation, with evocative questions and the low, breathy response of men pleasuring themselves.

"I'm not married," says a 25-year-old man who insists on anonymity. "I've got a girl, but we can't get together more than once a week. That leaves six days for solo sex. Sometimes you want to share it with somebody else. This party line stuff is the perfect answer."

We'll call him Jerry. It's usually around midnight when he phones, getting himself primed first to save money. He's gotten to know a few of the callers well, particularly the hostess.

"The great thing is, it's so private. I'm anybody I want to be—who's to know? I tell them I'm packing 10 inches, the girls moan and tell me what they'd like to do with it.

They describe themselves to me, all beautiful, young, big-breasted, So they're lying. So am I. We're playing sex games together, total strangers, getting off on each other. It's an orgy, talking dirty with people you don't even know, telling them what it feels like when you pump it. letting them hear you moan when you're coming, describing it to them. You don't think that's worth 10 or 15 bucks a week?"

Would he ever like to meet any of his telephone friends in person?

"No, that's exactly what I *don't* want. It's the impersonal thing that lets us be honest and free with each other. It's like making a legal obscene phone call."

For some, even speaking anonymously on the telephone to total strangers is too much of a challenge for their shyness. Some of them have found a solution in another electronic party line, HSX and similar computer forums through which people wanting to talk sex can meet. In this case, talk is anything but cheap. First, the would-be participant needs a modem, which translates computer signals into telephone signals and vice versa. And you'll need a computer. HSX, which stands for Human Sexuality, is accessed through compuServe, and offers what it calls Personals, Letters, Interactive Programs, and "Hot Lines," along with education programs.

These computer lines have a few advantages over the correspondence clubs. While you still have to write—or type—the chances are you're meeting a somewhat classier level or correspondent. This is too much of an investment of brains and money for your typical hustler or prostitute, and too cerebral for your typical postal inspector.

Unlike letters, but similar to the telephone party line, computer parties can include several participants. Instead of talking they write, and the screen might offer up a mass confusion as participants try to figure out who's saying what to whom.

And, like its telephone counterpart, when two people do manage to link up, they can agree to "talk," the computer command that will put them on their own private line. Then, you might get the sort of "conversation" described by Howard and Martha Lewis in their book, *The Electronic Confessional:*

Tony: "I want to make love to you. Will you let me?"

Julie: "Yes."

Tony: "I can see that you're beautiful. There's no reason to hold yourself back."

Julie: "I want you to touch me."

Tony: "Tell me where and how."

Julie: "I love having my nipples rubbed. Rub them slowly and gently."

And so forth, all the way to climax.

A man named Graham says he loves sex by computer because, "the computer has allowed me to commit adultery without being unfaithful to the woman I love."

Others admit frankly that they're physically unattractive, have high-pitched voices, stammer, have difficulty impressing people with their speech. Some women admit to enjoying flirtation and even sexual talk, but not wanting to go all the way.

"In the real world, if you told a man how much you like performing oral sex—I mean, if you said it just to turn him on, get him horny—the next thing you know you'd be gagging on you-know-what, and who can blame the guy?

On the computer, you can say whatever you want. But it's more like telling it to yourself, like in a diary. Suddenly there's some guy out there, maybe on the other side of the country, responding, and usualiy telling you just how he's responding."

I could never leave out this best testimony supporting computer sex: "The rugged, masculine men I like don't seem to be attracted to me. On the computer, once I tell them my tit size, how I love to suck cock and get fucked, they can't wait to get me in bed, so to speak. I've had sex with hundreds of them, and not one knows that the 'Debbie' they lust for is really a man!"

Are telephone and computer party lines worth the money? It depends on what you're after. If you want a safe opportunity for symbolic exhibitionism as part of a solo sex experience, if you want a real-live voyeur who enjoys the scene as much as you do, this is certainly one answer. The conversation you might have could be raunchy enough to make a porn star blush. But equally often it's a hodgepodge of mass confusion.

The key is in sampling the merchandise. Have several numbers available, and make up your mind quickly whether or not the conversation is going anywhere that interests you. If not, hang up and try another line.

Otherwise you could waste an hour's pay listening to a foxy lady whisper: "Hollo, somebody. Is anyone out there? Hello. Hello? Hello!"

THE JOY OF SOLO SEX

"The first step, then, is to
get people jerking off in pairs. I am
mystified why this is not as popular as it
should be. For me, mutual masturbation is
the hottest and most reciprocal sex act
two men can indulge in.
Hands can do more to and for a dick than
the anal sphincter can. One can watch
a cock being jerked off and watch it
come..."

—John Jackoff,
Gay Community News
August 2, 1987

Chapter 8
Fantasy Is More Real

FANTASIES ARE the most common sex activity known to man, much more than masturbation. When David Barlow, director of the Sexuality Research Program at the State University of New York in Albany, asked people to report every fantasy they had for several weeks, he found that "most people have about seven or eight fantasies a day, although the range can be from none to 40 and up."

A few years ago, 250 psychology students at Wayne University participated in another study. At unexpected moments during lectures over a nine-week period, the professor fired a gun loaded with blanks. Students were asked to write a brief note about what they were thinking at the moment the gunshot occurred. On average, 80 percent were paying no attention to the lecture. Instead, almost half of the daydreamers were entertaining sexual fantasies.

How often do you think about sex? Would you believe that sex crosses the mind of the average 12- to 25-year-old male once every other minute?

That was the finding of Paul Cameron, Ph.D., of the University of Louisville, when he interviewed more than 4,000 people from eight to 99 years old during all sorts of activities—frying eggs, watching a ball game, working. Sex thoughts decrease in frequency to about once every five minutes in middle age and once in ten after age 65 among men.

Women have fewer sex fantasies. They think about it two out of every five minutes during the teenage years, one in three during young adulthood and one in ten to 20 during the rest of their lives. Says Cameron, "Obviously every thought about sex is not a fantasy, but some substantial portion of such thoughts are."

If you have more sex fantasies than most men, or develop them in great detail, you probably have superior intelligence. N. Lukianowicz, M.D., writing in the *Archives of General Psychiatry,* reports that none of the 20 patients he interviewed who reported detailed sex fantasies had an IQ below 100; eight of them had IQs over 120 and one had an IQ of about 132. "Therefore," concludes Lukianowicz, "intelligence as such seems to have a positive influence on the occurrence of masturbatory fantasies. It is understandable that a dull individual has usually a poor imagery, and his masturbation is probably of the more primitive, tactile quality, without any emotional or imaginative accompaniment."

A few years ago, while I was counseling an 18-year-old boy who was suffering sexual guilt, he said to me, "I know guys have lots of sexual fantasies, but the ones I have most of the time are weird. I mean, they're just sick. I let them happen anyway, but when they're done and I come, I feel so ashamed."

I know you're wondering what his fantasies were, and I'll tell you as we go along, but the point is that young people in particular often feel that their fantasies are somehow perverted. As a result, they suffer guilt, which can affect negatively both their sex lives and their personalities in general. If they continue these fantasies, their self-esteem suffers. If they don't, they surrender what was obviously the source of very deep sexual pleasure. Neither is necessary, for, as we'll see, our fantasies are not uniquely ours. Whatever your fantasy, many millions share them harmlessly. Let me try to prove that.

According to studies by such researchers as Drs. Mark Schwartz, William Masters, David Barlow and Tom Anicar, the following are five of the most common fantasies we experience. I'll bet yours is among them.

1. The New Experience.

The most common type of sexual fantasy, according to Drs. Mark Schwartz and William Masters, who published their findings in the *American Journal of Psychiatry,* is having sex with someone other than your wife, steady girlfriend or steady guy.

Rick K., a 22-year-old Los Angeles student, reports a favorite example. Like most detailed fantasies, Rick's begins in reality. While in high school, he modeled nude for art classes to earn spending money. "When I'm kneeling up there bare-assed, some girl is finally going to get the hots so bad she won't be able to control it. She'll toss her clay against the wall and tackle me. Then all the others will join in, pulling off their panties and diddling themselves as they watch her play with my dick. They'll all get in line for a chance to do the same."

The ultimate fantasy of this sort centers around group sex. Two strangers knock on the door. Their car has broken down and they need help, which you, the fantasizer, offer—for a price: An uninhibited orgy. Or, you're invited to a party at which you find dozens of strangers having sex. You move from one partner to another all night long.

The key to understanding what New Experience fantasies say about you is that the partners are always strangers. It's not love you're looking for, just good, old-fashioned sex. Your real-life partner—or even the lack of a serious relationship—isn't troubling you. Only if and when your fantasy sex partner becomes important and romance becomes a part of the fantasy might you begin wondering whether your real-life relationship needs re-examining, say the experts.

2. Forced Encounters.

While such boy-gets-girl—or girls—fantasies are the most common, at least one daydream in four, according to the Schwartz-Masters study, is "deviant" in the sense that it would break social or legal codes if acted our in reality.

In fact, the second most common type of sexual fantasy centers around sadism, usually the daydreamer forcing his partner to submit to various acts with him. Women, too, find the idea appealing—in fantasy. Like the men, they listed it as their second most common sexual daydream.

"I have this thing—it really turns me on," says Carl B., a senior at Lehigh University in Bethlehem, Pennsylvania. "I tell Jill she's gotta prove she loves me, do anything I say, and she agrees. So I make her have sex with two of my buddies, right in front of me, and she's ashamed as hell but she does it. Licking, kissing, spreading, everything I say."

A novice at sexual fantasies might well feel guilt after entertaining and enjoying a rape or sadism fantasy (and self-appointed judges of the moral good will gleefully pile on their own condemnation). But Carl is a veteran fantasizer, and he's discovered for himself what psychiatrists report to be generally true.

What turns Carl on in the wonderful world of make-believe would be a disaster in reality. "First," he says, "I don't want anybody else screwing with Jill. I'm the jealous type. Besides, I can't get into sex unless she's into it, too. I tried once when she was depressed. I just couldn't do it. That's what is so neat about fantasies—you can do what you don't want to do in *reality*, and you can make it turn out just perfect."

According to Dr. Barlow, Carl is typical of those whose sexual imaginations tend toward the kinky. "For most people who have a fantasy of rape," he says, "it's a very idealized, even romantic act, something like the rape scene in *The Fantasticks*." He adds, "In our research, we find that if you play a tape for them of a realistic description of a rape, with all its pain and violence, they don't get aroused."

You may find it interesting to know that men who fantasize raping sometimes switch their make-believe identity to that of the rape victim. (You'll recall my comments about the real rapist identifying with his victim's terror as a means of experiencing danger in a second-hand, cowardly way.) In rape fantasies, however, as compared to the act in reality, the daydreamer-as-victim gets to surrender helplessly to a partner whose entire purpose is to give his "victim" pleasure. In fantasy, the rapist is overwhelmed by his victim's beauty and sexuality, so much so that he loses control of himself because you are so irresistible.

Remember we're talking about fantasy here. If you can't make that distinction, you're missing the whole point.

The real life rapist suffers a sense of inferiority in dealing on an equal basis with women—or men, depending upon his orientation. Only when his sexual partner is forced into submission by threats on his or her life, or, in more violent situations, actually brutalized, can a rapist have a sense of masculine dominance and potency. But many millions of people simply can't be wrong; in fantasy, being attacked because of their sexual desirability can be a pleasant trip.

I want to add a bit about dominance or control fantasies. In at least two cases, they can signify emotional problems. The first involves violent, even murderous sadism, or "eroticized hatred" in the words of Dr. Robert Stoller.

Millions of men also have occasional fantasies in which the sexual partner is adolescent or younger. When such fantasies are exclusive of all others, it says that the fantasizer can't feel in sexual control when relating to adult partners. While you can't go to jail for what you're thinking, as the song says, a steady diet of pedophile fantasies can chip away at the legal/moral armor that keeps most of us from acting out our sexual daydreams. More to the point, sex therapist all over the country are teaching men how to feel sexual power in more acceptable ways.

As you probably know, there is a raging controversy going on about whether violent pornography (or pedophile-oriented, or homosexually-oriented, or what-ever) leads to actual acting out in the real world. Obviously, the same question should be raised about fantasy. The evidence that pornography (and, by implication, fantasy) does lead to acting out rests primarily on the fact that many mass murderers had in their libraries dozens of books fictionally depicting the crimes they committed. Did reading that material push them over the edge, forcing them to act out in reality what proved so satisfying in the world of make-believe?

The argument seems to make sense. But I have personally know several men who have had truly huge collections of sadomasochistic books and magazines, and who have admitted being consumed with such fantasies, but who have insisted that they found the idea of acting out S&M fantasies in reality utterly repugnant. Statistically, millions of men fit into this category. While violence in fantasy and pornography acts as a release of pent-up tension, real-life violence is abhorrent to them.

My experience in this matter leads me to the conclusion that we all read what we want to read and fantasize what turns us on. Normal people, even those violent by nature, use pornography as a safety valve—although they are usually not aware that they're doing so. Once they experience orgasm through a fantasy scene, their passions are spent until next time, and as long as the safety valve works, the pornography or fantasy actually postpones at worst, and totally replaces at best, the need for acting out in the real world. It is simply silly to believe that a pedophile, for example, never thought of having sex with a child until he read about it in a book which he unintentionally stumbled across and found lust-producing. Most men are aware of their sexual orientation early in their teenage years, at least on a very fundamental level.

Certainly pedophiles, sadists, and rapists have their sexual identities imprinted by the time they're in their mid-teens, long before they read pornography, for the most part. I have personally interviewed men who insist that, had it *not* been for pornography, they certainly would have been forced to commit sexual crimes. The pornography, and the fantasies it triggers, allow the crime to be lived out in a safe yet fulfilling way. The attack on pornography is generally a cheap political trick designed to get votes. At best it is a sincere and stupid effort to protect society from that which is not only innocent but probably extremely beneficial.

The same is true of your fantasies.

Nonetheless—and here is the point you should remember—some fantasies show limited development of one's sexuality when they are enjoyed exclusively. Although you may not think it true now, your sex life can be much more brilliant in its variety and splendor, and contribute significantly to your overall emotional health, if you allow it to develop in a fuller, more mature way. Perhaps you will need professional help. In any case, it's worth the effort.

3. Voyeurism.

Here's a fantasy that one young man swears has brought him approximately 1,000 orgasms in the past five years; these are his words:

> I came home from work early one day last week, hoping to surprise my wife, Alise. I thought I'd take her to lunch and a movie or something but she wasn't home. So I put on the TV, and it was about an hour before Alise walked in the door. Her hair was messed up a little, her cheeks were red, her lips a little swollen. She had that look in her

eyes—the way she always gets when she's had a few good orgasms.

"What the hell's going on?" I yelled.

She could tell by my face there was no sense lying.

"I've been with John," she told me with a casual shrug. John's my best friend. I felt the anger welling up, the heat flushing my face. I got this hollow feeling in my stomach. But she reached out and pulled me to her. Then she began to kiss me all over my face.

"He's got such a big, beautiful dick," she told me while unbuckling my belt. Then, fondling me, she told me detail by detail how she couldn't resist him, how she was the one who started it. She explained how she knelt in front of him and did just what she was doing to me, how she played with his body, kissing every part of it, taking him into her mouth. I got so hot I couldn't stand it, started asking her questions about what it was like when he climbed on her....

Actually, none of that ever happened in real life. But that doesn't mean it's not real. It happens about once a week in this young man's head, a few details changing here and there, and it's as vivid and real as any flesh and blood sex scene he's ever experienced, and at least as satisfying.

As male sexual fantasies go, that's actually a rather common and tame example: Voyeurism (he "observes" the sex between Alice and John), psychic masochism (he is forced into the humility of watching his best friend and girl ignore him and enjoy each other sexually), and homosexuality (as he identifies with Alice in making love to John). These are among the most common types of erotic make-believe.

In fact, the Peeping Tom daydream is the third most popular among both men and women.

"There's this girl in the house across the street," says Dave D., a computer technician in a Philadelphia suburb. "The most I've ever seen of her was when she came into the living room one night in a bra and panties to close the curtains. But in my fantasy she forgets about the curtains and even the bra and panties and makes out right there by the window with her boyfriend.

"Sometimes I get the girl who lives in the apartment above me into it, too—in my fantasy, I mean. She watches them, too, and gets so hot she throws off her clothes and starts playing with herself. Then I'm outside watching all three of them, and they're watching me and each other."

"They're all co-ed dorms here," says a junior at a New Jersey university. "Every now and then a girl in that dorm over there will pull off her sweater and forget to pull down the shades. I never saw any tits or anything like that, but that's my fantasy. She strips. Her boyfriend comes in, and they make out. I watch the whole thing."

Voyeuristic fantasies are an indication of creativity and imagination. They're simply the garden variety New Experience fantasy with a twist—in his daydream, the student identifies with the man he's watching. Not only does he have all the pleasures of sex with a beautiful woman, but he gets to admire his vicarious self at the same time—sort of like watching himself in a mirror while he has sex.

4. Homosexual Fantasies.

Surprisingly common among straight men are fantasies of sex with other men. In fact, they're fourth most popular. (They're even more popular among women, according to psychiatrist Sonja Freeman.)

About 80 percent of all males have such fantasies, according to Alfred Kinsey—and most men feel guilty about them. Yet, this is a safe and harmless means of expressing our natural bisexuality without actually acting it out in reality. Exploring such fantasies is much more healthy emotionally than suppressing those feelings.

From childhood on, most males have a fascination with other men's genitals. It begins with secret explorations of their best friends' bodies, reaching the mutual masturbation phase in adolescence. In adulthood, perfectly heterosexual men seek out porn flicks with super-endowed studs. Why? Usually, it's not so much a desire for other men as sex partners as a normal fascination with male genitals, their various shapes and sizes, that leads many men to explore gay sex play in magazines, films and fantasies.

None of us would want to meet King Kong face-to kneecap, or confront Rosemary's weird brat in person, or to watch the Godfather's henchmen spill blood and brains all over the sidewalk. We enjoy pornography and sexual fantasy, as we do films of horror and violence, precisely because they're unreal. Unlike reality, it all turns out well in the end. After the illusion serves its purpose, either to entertain or produce orgasm, we can go back to our ordinary lives without facing the consequences of troubled conscience.

I do not mean to suggest that any man *should* have a troubled conscience as a result of enjoying sex with another man. In fact, it is my personal belief—having studied extensively both the historical and anthropological data, carefully examining modern social-sexual behavior and interviewing hundreds of men regarding their secret sexual fantasies and behavior—that nine men in ten have either a conscious or suppressed desire to have sex with another man. Apart from theological teachings (for which I have great respect), there can be no persuasive argument against fulfilling those desires in a safe, disease-free way. But prejudices are not rational, and the great majority of men have a prejudice not only against sex with other males, but against such fantasies. They entertain them, of course, but afterward they often feel a great sense of guilt. It is for those readers that I stress the fact that such fantasies are so common that men who don't have them are in the great minority and therefore according to some definitions of the norm are themselves the deviates.

Some men have found a clever way of dealing with the guilt about gay fantasies: They simply add a woman to the scene, thereby making it a heterosexual fantasy in which the gay sex is demanded by the woman in order to please her. If that adaptational approach works, I certainly encourage it.

Here's a detailed example of such a fantasy from Anthony Crowell's *The Body Abusers.* In this elaborate fantasy, a man in his late teens has been making love to his sister Nancy for several years. Eventually she marries Marvin, who, like the brother, is submissive and obeys her every wish. She tells Marvin about her relationship with her brother and arranges to have both men service her at the same time.

...we went into the bedroom and she made us all undress. She went after Marvin and blew him before he even had a chance to sit down....

When she sort of slaked her thirst she wanted us both on the bed with her. She made me screw her while she was up on her hands and knees and while I was screwing her she was blowing Marvin again....

When she finally collapsed on him, panting and heaving with the pleasures of her big orgasm, she just lay there and we all got some rest but only for about a half hour. Then she made Marvin go down on me and he began sucking me as capably as she did it, but she kept telling him not to let me pop. She wanted to do that herself. His mouth and tongue began driving me out of my skull and she kept watching us very closely, and just when I was about to explode, he slid his mouth off my dick and she grabbed it and popped it herself.

Later she made me do the same thing to Marvin and I sort of enjoyed doing that to Marvin. I had never thought that I would, but I did. Nancy kept both of us drained dry that night and when we finally did go to sleep we were all exhausted and drained dry.

That weekend set the pattern for our life together. She had gotten a dildo somewhere and she used that to sodomize both of us and she took great pleasure in doing that to us, probably because while she was sodomizing me, Marvin was sucking me off, and when she was sodomizing him, I had to do it to him. That became a regular practice because she got some sort of perverted pleasure out of making us suck each other. Sometimes she'd make us do a sixty-nine while she sat and watched us.

5. Exhibitionism.

When Tom Anicar, in preparation for his book *Secret Sex—Male Erotic Fantasies,* processed many thousands of responses from males across the country, he found that most fantasies centered around making the woman worship and revere the male sex organ.

In some fantasies, two women—or a host of them— perform the ritual of phallic adoration and worship. And one of the most exciting ideas in the American male mind is having sex in front of an audience.

"In my fantasy, I'm the young ruler of a great empire, another Alexander the Great," says a handsome blond technician in his mid-20's. "I have decided to select a wife and I've spread word throughout the kingdom. She will have all the wealth she could ever dream of. She will have servants and every pleasure she craves. She may choose any man, woman or child in the kingdom to satisfy her sexual cravings—I am not the jealous type. But she must battle for the privilege of marrying me.

"I publish the rules of the contest. The women must be young and voluptuous, with large tits. They must gather in the courtyard beneath the balcony of my palace. They must be naked, hard cock in hand, and slowly begin massaging it. As it swells, the nude women begin tearing at each other, fighting for a position beneath the balcony with their faces uplifted and mouths wide open. Only the woman who catches my sperm in her mouth shall be my bride.

"Screaming, clawing at each other's bodies with their fingernails, trampling each other under foot, they fight valiantly for the sacred fluid. One after another they fall bleeding to the ground, some stomped, kicked, beaten.

"The more the organ swells, the more turgid it becomes, the more violently they attack each other. All through the crowd faces are uplifted, mouths gaping.

"In the moment of ejaculation, bodies lunge, bruised tits bobbing, thighs and bellies gyrating against each other. One woman hurls herself into the air, her body bloody, her mouth thrust open to catch the splash of semen.

"Immediately she collapses, but my guards rescue her and she is prepared for the marriage ceremony."

According to John P. Callan, M.D., an authority on human sexuality, exhibitionism (whether in fact or fantasy) is a way of reassuring ourselves of our sexual power. Teenage males in particular, lacking experience with women, bolster their confidence that women will be impressed with their sex organs through phallic-oriented fantasies.

If exhibitionistic fantasies are your thing, go with them. There's nothing wrong with needing assurance, either that your body is attractive or that your sex organs are potent and impressive.

I've discussed here the most common fantasies, but that list of five is by no means exhaustive. A complete list of fantasies held by ordinary, emotionally healthy people would probably be literally without limit, since young people are maturing every day, and every human being has a unique and new imagination. Some of the fantasies that will strike many people as outrageous and yet are not rare include these which have been reported to me repeatedly by many men:

I have sex with a child.

Some street punks make me suck them off while they cut off my cock and balls.

I castrate my girlfriend's secret lover.

My lover and I leap out of a plane and have sex while plunging to our deaths.

I make out with a German Shepherd (the four-legged variety).

She strangles me while I am making love to her and am in the throes of orgasm.

The key to achieving expertise in the art of generating sexual fantasy at its best is complete honesty with yourself. You must be willing to say to yourself, "This is what I like, what excites me, whether or not it's shameful to others. In real life I would not do this, but the truth (which you may keep your own secret) is that nothing turns me on as much as this 'kinky,' 'deviant,' 'perverted' fantasy." If you can be that honest about yourself without feeling threatened, you are a long way toward getting more out of fantasy than most men do.

The second thing you want to keep in mind grows directly from this capacity to be honest with yourself: The sexual areas that cause you the most anxiety can in fantasy absolutely blow your mind with pleasure. Here's an example:

"I'm 30 years old. My first wife and I had great sex, three times a day for years. When we divorced and I remarried, I guess some of that old fundamentalist guild came to the surface—you're not supposed to remarry if you're a fundamentalist. Anyway, I had a hell of a time getting a hard on with my second wife. I felt like shit. She was beautiful, but I just couldn't get it up for her. And of course that kind of thing reinforces itself.

"I felt crushed, not even a man. I was getting into a real depression. Then one day while I was laying next to my wife in bed, I started thinking she'd have to get another guy to satisfy her. That was my greatest fear, but instead of running away from it I let it play out.

"He was there in bed with us, a perfect athlete, and they were hot as hell for each other. They looked at my puny dick and laughed at me, and then he slid his big cock into her and slowly began fucking her. They were moaning and groaning, completely ignoring me, and before I knew it, the whole thing was so real I was ignoring me, too. I got a screaming erection, rolled over on top of my wife and became the other guy. I was looking at the puny dick laying next to us and showing him how it ought to be done, riding her like a real stud. It was the best orgasm either of us had ever had.

"I don't use the fantasy much—I don't want to wear it out. But whenever I feel the tension coming on, I let myself slip back into it, admitting that I can't be a man and letting this other stud do it for me."

The reason death is often associated with sex and orgasm is precisely this: *our greatest fears can be translated into our most intense pleasures if we confront them with vivid imagination.* I have been told more than once by perfectly heterosexual men for example that many of their most thrilling fantasies centered on being taken and used and pleasured by force by a gang of very masculine men. Others, as described on page 119, have sex-and-death fantasies, and still others fantasize their lovers leaving them for more sexual desirable partners. In each case, these are all but unbearable fears translated to pleasure through the power of sex.

In the next chapter you'll learn a skill few men have mastered—how to be absorbed so deeply in your fantasy that it will be more intense than your real life. Here's how to have fantasies more potent than you ever dreamed possible.

Chapter 9
Ultimate Fantasies

THE ULTIMATE fantasy is an imaginary experience that is more vivid and real than any dream. It is like being transported mentally from where you are to where you want to be. It involves auto-suggestion, or self-hypnosis, and requires intense concentration to the point of being completely absorbed in sex.

Sweeping the stage

Right now, even as you read this book, a jumble of unconscious thoughts and distractions are probably flittering through your mind. If that isn't true of you personally, you are an exceptional individual with unusual powers of concentration. You're most likely a faster reader than most—perhaps even a speed reader. You might already understand instinctively the art of concentration.

The first step in concentrating—in this particular case on our sexual fantasies—is to clear our heads of all distractions. Believe it or not, sweeping our *mental* stages clean begins with eliminating tension from our bodies. That's because your body and mind are not separate entities, but the body in some ways actually is a part of the mind, and vice versa. For example, cold, damp weather makes us emotionally moody because our bodies are uncomfortable. On the other hand, our emotional problems can cause serious physical illness, including intolerable pain. These are called psychosomatic, or body-mind ailments. But even that term implies two distinct entities.

Failure to recognize the oneness of the body/mind is probably the major reason that some people can't relax completely. Tension in the body is tension in the mind. You can't sleep if your muscles are tense. You can't enjoy the intensity of the orgasm if you are tense, either. And you certainly can't concentrate on a sexual fantasy so deeply that it becomes completely real to you.

Sweeping the mental stage clean begins with relaxing the body's muscles. The four primary muscle tension groups of the body are the legs, abdomen, back, and neck/shoulders. The best way to relax them is through stretch exercises. Here are the ones which I believe are the most effective.

Sitting Toe Touch

Sitting on the floor with your legs outstretched, feet together, reach for your toes. If you aren't very flexible, you probably won't be able to do this at first. Don't strain, just reach. After about a minute, those stubborn, tense muscles in your back and lower calves will begin to relax. As they do, lean farther forward. If you're particularly stiff, you won't reach your toes the first day, perhaps not the second.

When you do, you're halfway to the final goal, which is to touch your forehead to your knees. Long before that you will feel the benefits of stretching and relaxing those back, shoulder and leg muscles.

Back Bend

Start in a kneeling position. Slowly and carefully lean back. The object is to touch the back of your head to the

126

floor. This must be done carefully and cautiously, for the quadriceps (upper thigh muscles) of most people are not used to being stretched, and a fast movement can tear them. This exercise is wonderful for stretching thigh muscles and those of the chest, neck and abdomen.

Head Rotation

The most obvious sites of tension in most people are the muscles of the shoulders and back that extend into the neck. We just don't give these muscles much exercise, and the result is that when they grow tight with tension they remain that way. The best exercise for stretching and relaxing them is the old-fashioned head roll.

Drop your head sideways toward your left shoulder. (Unless you're more flexible than most, your head won't reach the shoulder.) Let it droop there, allowing the muscles to stretch.

Roll your head back. slowly and gently, careful not to tear tight muscles. After a stretching period, roll your head over the right shoulder and pause. Finally, let it hang forward.

Repeat the exercise five times, then reverse the direction.

When you've attained flexibility in the major muscle groups, the next step is *progressive physical relaxation.* It's the most effective method of muscle relaxation I know, yet it takes only a few minutes.

Progressive relaxation is based on the simple fact that you can't consciously relax a muscle unless you're consciously aware that it's tense. When you *feel* the tension in the muscle, you can deliberately relax it.

Make your hand into a fist. Clench the fist for three seconds, then slowly relax it and let your hand and arm go limp. Repeat it twice, then do it twice with the other hand.

That exercise was introductory only, to give you an idea of what we'll be doing with all the muscles of your body. Now, close your eyes. Concentrate on the muscles of your forehead, tightening them as much as you can. Don't cheat—make them *really* tight. Maintain the tension for three seconds, then let those muscles relax.

Move on to your jaw muscles, then your neck, shoulders, arms, torso, buttocks, legs, feet.

If you don't feel a dramatic release of tension as you relax the muscles, repeat the exercise—and continue the repetitions, concentrating on both the tension and relaxation, until the muscles do relax.

And you *will* relax. Much of the muscle tension we endure results from our not being consciously aware of the tension. Many of us go through each day with our muscles unconsciously contracted in preparation for battle, but since most of our enemies in modern life are emotional and psychological, we never get the opportunity to use those muscles and then relax them. Instead, they're in a chronic state of tension, and only by exaggerating that tension can we become aware of it and allow them to relax.

Once your body is relaxed, the next step is to relax your mind. You will need a *Perfect Peace Scene*. Try to recall a time and place of perfect serenity. Perhaps it was when you were a child gazing up at the stars on a warm summer night, or lying on a beach while the waves splashed a few feet away, or resting near the trunk of a tall tree in a towering forest. Perhaps you can recall being a child in your mother's comforting arms, falling asleep in her lap. Decide upon your *Perfect Peace Scene* now.

Let me stress there should be no erotic content to this scene. Its purpose is not to stir fantasy images but to clear all images whatever from your mind. That's why you want to choose the most relaxing scene you can recall.

After you've completely relaxed the muscles of your body, find a place where you can sit or recline comfortably without the likelihood of being interrupted or distracted by outside noises or activities. The room should be relatively dark. If you want background music, make sure it's soft and non-intrusive.

Lie there quietly. Now, without any effort of the will, allow your *Perfect Peace Scene* to grow clear in your mind. Simply let it take place—don't try to force it. Such an act of the intellect adds clutter to the mind's stage rather than clearing it.

Allow yourself to dissolve into the scene. See the colors. Smell the pine needles. Listen to the waves or crackling fire or music. Feel the sand on your mother's arms or the carpet or the earth beneath you.

With practice you'll be able to reach that special place in your mind in 30 seconds to a minute, and once there, the outside world won't distract you from it.

Now you're ready to empty your mind completely. Think of a passive, tranquil color. Light blue or pale green work best for me. Perhaps you will prefer gray or soft beige. Allow the vision of your tranquil place to dissolve slowly in the color until there is nothing...nothing but that hue in your mind.

When you reach the point where you have absolutely no thoughts floating around in your head, not even the thought that you have no thoughts, but when your whole mind is filled with the color you've chosen, you're ready for a solo sex experience relatively few men have known. I don't recommend that you take the following steps the first time out. You'll probably be disappointed because, as has been the case in each chapter of this book, the following steps, if they are to be successful, require perfecting what has come before. In this case, it is wiser to perfect the relaxation techniques I've already discussed until you are in complete control of them and can go into the state of perfect relaxation with the absence of thought before moving on to the more complex and rewarding sexual imagery.

Creating the Living Image

When most of us think about a subject, or fantasize a sexual scene, our minds work like a floodlight, bathing a large area with a moderate brightness. Now that your mind is free of thoughts, you can do better than that. You can fantasize like a spotlight, concentrating on a relatively small area but with an intensity so bright that it reveals every detail. You are going to experience what I call *sensory intensity,* which means that you will heighten in your imagination each of the senses that come into play in your fantasy.

Step One. Select an erotic scene, situation or individual. Let's pretend that you've chosen to watch a beautiful couple make love.

Step Two. Follow the total relaxation techniques we've just discussed until your mind is empty, the stage a soft and passive shade of green, blue, gray or whatever color you've chosen. Continue in this relaxation phase until your mind is free of all thought.

Step Three. Focus on the pre-selected scene you've chosen, in our example that of an attractive naked couple making love. Don't force the scene; allow it to emerge at its own pace from the solid color that fills your mind. Watch the skin color appear on that soft-hued background...the shape of the bodies grow distinct. Move in closer to observe the skin. You can actually see the pores, the moisture forming on the bodies. Move so close that you can smell the bodies, hear the two bodies smacking together with each thrust, see the sweat trickling between breasts and buttocks, dripping from testicles.

Bring into play all your senses. What do you see, in detail? Listen not only to the moaning, but to all the sounds—the panting, the scraping of nails against sheets, sweaty breast against breast. You can hear the sound of fucking.

There are many smells: The natural odors of the bodies, perfume, cologne, musky, fresh. Even the clean bed linen has its own smell.

Do you want to taste the sweat on the bodies? The lips of either or both lovers? These are your performers. You have created them to do your bidding.

Enjoy them as you wish. Taste them freely.

Touch them, too. Run your fingers along the sweat-drenched legs. Feel the matted hair, the silky skin, the strong muscles. Touch whatever parts of their bodies you like, not with your intellect or will, but with your senses. *Really* feel them.

"The all-time best sex experience I ever had was—I was gonna say it was by myself," says a 22-year-old New Jersey truck driver. "But I wasn't alone. I was with two women and another guy. Sure, they were figments of my imagination if you want to call it that. But I swear, I felt those people, smelled the bodies—it was as real as any sex I ever had. That was a couple years ago, and today it's hard for me to believe it didn't really happen. It was that real."

You won't need any testimonials to convince you after your first experience with ultimate fantasizing. Even if you aren't entirely successful in your first couple of attempts, your "failures" will be of a much richer and rewarding quality than the fantasies you've known until now.

If you should continue to have problems in getting completely absorbed in the fantasy, here are some possible reasons:

1. You're rushing things, allowing your intellect and will to dominate. Think of the will (or intellect) and your imagination as two phone lines coming in to the same receiver. You can use either one or the other, but you can't use both simultaneously. The system just doesn't work that way. As soon as you give control to the will, the imagination ceases to function.

2. Imagination plays a major part in *sensory intensity*. Unfortunately, some of us are not gifted with highly active imaginations. If that's the case with you, you might find it difficult to create as vivid and detailed a mental picture as you would like. The key is to keep a checklist in the recesses of your mind with the following words: *sight, sound, smell, taste, touch*. Do not concentrate on this list, or you will allow the intellect to crowd out the imagin-

ation. Instead, leave it there off-stage, and refer to it only when necessary. Move gracefully and without pressure through each of these categories, and by the time you're finished creating all the details in your imagination, you'll have the most vivid fantasy of your life.

Controlling the Fantasy

In my experience, most men have a preconceived agenda concerning where they want their sexual fantasies to go. For example, "I want to watch a beautiful woman with big tits masturbate herself," or "I want a tall, muscular man to make me lick his balls." Directing sex fantasies of the vivid, completely imaginative and almost preconscious sort, those which we're talking about here, along such specific lines is certainly possible. But it's quite difficult, and might not even be desirable. Here's what I mean:

I've already talked about the conflict between the intellect and the imagination. Keep in mind that when you are in this very deep level of fantasy it's almost like a state of semi-sleep. Your mind is completely relaxed, and to intrude upon that state by willfully directing the imagination to take a specific course is to risk "breaking the spell," so to speak. The fantasy can continue, but usually on a shallow, everyday level.

Some people *have* perfected the art of subtly nudging their imaginations into certain directions, however, and you might wish to experiment with that after perfecting the previous stages of intense fantasizing. Don't be disappointed if, while learning, you find even the most superficial fantasies illusive. You must learn to control without controlling, and that will take time. One approach that has proven successful is to narrow the scope of the erotic scene with which you begin. For example, if there is a particular part of a lover's anatomy upon which you wish to concentrate, start by focusing specifically on that, along with any details that will play a part in the fantasy you wish to experience.

For the patient sexualist, non-directed stream-of-consciousness fantasies will ultimately prove more satisfying. One reason is that they're new and fresh, even to the fantasizer, for they reach down into his unconscious for the material we rarely even know is there, but which can trigger the very most passionate thrills. Such fantasies are not only more real than real, but they have a life of their own and can be full of surprises. Sometimes they go absolutely nowhere—you find yourself absorbed in almost a photograph, a three dimensional still-life. Perhaps your whole mind is filled with an intensely close, pulsating sex organ or anatomical detail. At other times, bizarre sexual embraces flitter across the stage of your mind. These experiences can be sexual adventures.

Whichever type of fantasy you enjoy most of the time, you'll want to spend at least some time in a non-directed, free-flowing fantasy state. That's because the ultimate experience, the psychic orgasm, in which concentration is riveted on pure, detached, psychic lust, grows form this unconscious drifting.

So, go ahead. Using information and anecdotes from pervious chapters, or drawing upon your own imagination, create a sexual scene or situation into which you're eager to delve. Don't hesitate to commit a couple of hours to achieving perfect physical and mental relaxation—as we stressed in the first chapters, you deserve it. There are few undertakings in life as rewarding as good solo sex. Then, when you're completely relaxed, let the scene develop, growing out of the mist of your chosen color and unfolding in all its sensory delight.

And when the time comes that you can endure the breathless tension no more, feel free to bring yourself naturally and beautifully to orgasm.

But I predict that a few of you will endure the tension longer, breathlessly allowing it to mount until without even touching your penis you will have the mind-blowing and quite rare experience of orgasm without any physical stimulation at all. Most of you will know that thrill after further instruction in following chapters, but those of you who experience it now are but a hair's breath from the true psychic orgasm.

"Sexuality is not a leisure or part-time activity.   It is a way of being."

—Alexander Lowen, *Love and Orgasm*

"Just as sexual energy had helped man out of his spiritual state into the body, so it can help him to return in full awareness to his devine primal state of wholeness."

—Elizabeth Haich, *Sexual Energy and Yoga*

Chapter 10
How to Have Multiple Orgasms

HE WAS a young man, in his early 20's, an ordinary-looking guy who would never catch your attention in a crowd. Yet, he claimed to have a very special talent. Two sex researchers had heard about him, Dr. Mina Robbins, professor of human development at California State University at Sacramento, and Dr. Gordon Jensen, professor of psychiatry and pediatrics at the University of California, Davis.

Robbins and Jenson wanted absolute proof. They invited the guy and his girl to their laboratory. First, they attached to various parts of his body devices for recording respiratory rate, pulse, muscle tension, urethral and anal contractions, penile firmness and brain waves. They then let the couple alone in a room with a bed.

Within half an hour they knew the man had been telling the truth. First, he reached what he had called a "preliminary" orgasm, with the intense thrill of a typical orgasm, but without ejaculation and lacking the final, ultimate fulfillment. His erection lessened slightly for about 20 seconds. Then, all the readings indicated that he began building toward another orgasm.

Each orgasm lasted for about one minute, much longer than most men experience. He would have four or five of them, followed by the most intense orgasm, with ejaculation and total fulfillment. Only then did he lose libido, or sex interest.

Even with such scientific evidence as this, Carol Tavris, a social psychologist, says that "the news is being greeted the same way that news about the female multiple was: 'I don't believe it.' 'It's a medical impossibility.' 'Oh, hell.'"

But the renowned sex therapist Wardell Pomeroy, Ph.D., writing in the physicians' journal *Medical Aspects of Human Sexuality,* answers the question, "Is multiple climax by males a fiction?" by saying: "If we can arbitrarily define multiple orgasm in the male as having more than one orgasm in less than 20 minutes, then over half of pre-adolescent males have had this experience. By age 15, 20 percent of the males will have multiple orgasms, and even by age 60 there are still one percent of the males who will experience this."

"Multiple orgasm" originally described an occasional experience exclusive to women. Here's what happens, according to William Masters, M.D., and Virginia Johnson, in their classic *Human Sexual Response:*

"First, the female is capable of rapid return to orgasm immediately following an orgasmic experience if restimulated before tensions have dropped below plateau-phase response levels [where sexual tension dissipates]. Second, the female is capable of maintaining an orgasmic experience for a relatively long period of time...from 20 to more than 60 seconds..."

Richard B. Lower, M.D., reported on several college students who masturbated 10 to 12 times a day (we referred to his study earlier). Another researcher, Alexander Lowen, M.D., had a patient who experienced 22 orgasms daily. Yet, none of these men were true examples of multiple orgasm, it seems. That's because they did not maintain erections between orgasms, nor did they have several orgasms within minutes, as is true of the multiple orgasms of women.

Men who have learned to be multi-orgasmic—and it can be learned—are not really all that rare. William Hartman, M.D., and Marilyn Fithian, co-directors of the Center for Marital and Sexual Study in Long Beach, California, have monitored 33 of them in the laboratory and have confirmed that during a single sexual session they averaged four orgasms each. Some had only two, and one man had 16.

Researchers Robbins and Jensen may have documented the male multiple orgasm record when one of their subjects, 49 years old, decided to see how far he could go. He surpassed 25, each of them lasting one full minute.

In response to an article I recently authored on the subject of multiple orgasm, one young man from Mesa, Arizona, wrote to me of his experience:

"I am a multi-orgasmic male. I am 28 years of age and have been married four and one half years now. Today my wife called Sally Jesse Rafael, who is a well known syndicated radio psychologist, and asked her if any research has or is being done on men such as myself. You see, it hasn't been long that I learned that I was rather unique among most men, yet despite my attempts to contact the Kinsey Institute and Masters and Johnson, I have still been unable to learn anything about the 'condition.' In fact, I was treated very rudely over the phone and was told they were not interested. My wife related this to Sally and she seemed quite perplexed and unable to understand why I received such a harsh reception.

"Anyway, to make a long story short, she told my wife that you were conducting a survey on multi-orgasmic men. So I'm writing in.

"Unlike some men I have heard about, I do not need to withhold ejaculation nor am I a premature ejaculator. In fact I have never had any sexual dysfunctions of any kind whatsoever, nor am I a sex addict. I've only made love to my wife and was a virgin before we met, despite an intense sex drive.

"I am able to maintain an erection through as many orgasms as I desire, whether that be two, or 20. On the average I have between five and 10 orgasms a day, and usually between two to five per love making session. I do not have a refractory period.

"After a few orgasms, depending on the position, exhaustion naturally wears me down (pun intended) but only long enough for me to catch my breath, assuming I wish more. No physical or mental stimulation is necessary."

You probably already know more than you realize about how men like this fellow achieve multiple orgasms. *Orgasms are primarily mental, not physiological experiences.* That's why paraplegics, with no sensations below the waist, can experience orgasms. It is why men whose genitals have been removed can do the same.

You don't think so? Writing in *Medical Aspects of Human Sexuality*, Milton T. Edgerton, M.D., who has performed many male-to-female sex change operations, says, "It has been the experience of the Gender Identity Clinic at the University of Virginia Medical Center that approximately 60 percent of all patients who are converted from male anatomy to female anatomy as a result of transsexual operations report repeated and successful attainment of orgasm with sexual experience. Patients are emphatic about this history and it is confirmed that this is true by their partners. In some instances, the patients reach orgasm in 100 percent of the reported attempts."

That's because, although we typically experience orgasm and ejaculation (along with complete fulfillment and loss of desire) simultaneously, the two are actually under separate neurological controls. Julian M. Davidson, professor of physiology at Stanford University, writes in *Psychology Today,* "Activation of neurons in the septum, a part of the limbic system at the top of the brain stem, is reportedly associated with orgasm. Two areas in the spinal cord in the middle and lower back apparently coordinate the mechanics of ejaculation, including the movement of semen into the urethra and the contractions that ejaculate it..."

Once ejaculation takes place, virtually all men lose sexual interest, at least temporarily. Says Davidson of multi-orgasmic men, "They experience the orgasmic ASC [altered state of consciousness] along with the penile contractions that ordinarily lead to ejaculation, but they ejaculate only with the final orgasm and then become sexually satiated." Although this isn't true of *all* multi-orgasmic men (the man extensively quoted above has act-ual ejaculations with each of his orgasms), it certainly is valid for the majority.

Orgasm occurs in the mind. The goal, therefore, is to concentrate on the "preliminary," or mini-orgasms, to enjoy each of them for as long as possible, but to back off before flipping over the edge to inevitable full climax.

"I can only do it when I'm really hot and want to spend a lot of time in sex," says a writer in his late 20's. "I mean, you've got to enjoy the play part, too, not just getting the big O. That's the idea, of course. If you were satisfied, why would you want to keep going at it and get other orgasms? But that's the whole thing right there—do you want a lot of little ones that aren't quite all that you can feel? do you just want to go on playing the game, having lots of little ones first?"

An important distinction needs to be made here between the multiple orgasms of teenagers described by Pomeroy and those experienced by many thousands of adults like this writer. Pomeroy is talking about the normal psycho-physiological recovery rate required by men before they are capable of experiencing new lust and erection. (I use the word lust deliberately; it's a good, healthy, clearly understood word for which we needn't apologize.)

Men are put together in such fashion that the complete orgasm, which is the goal of their lust, satisfies and dissipates desire. When the lust goes, so does the erection in most adult men. However, two factors can change that.

* In some males, primarily but not exclusively the young, erectile function is so spontaneous that even as desire wanes erections remain firm. Even if the penis becomes somewhat soft or even completely flaccid, it can be restored to firmness quickly with any kind of contact stimulation. In these cases, men can perform intercourse again quickly, even when libido isn't particularly aroused. They might even reach orgasm without having any particular interest in sex, a strictly physiological response.

Those are the multiple orgasms about which Pomeroy wrote.

* The multiple orgasms about which we're concerned here come about by maintaining a high libido or lust level. While Pomeroy's repeatedly orgasmic men ejaculate and have a full orgasmic experience each time, the libido-directed multiple orgasms depend on *avoiding* ejaculation and complete fulfillment except for the final event. That's because for most of us complete fulfillment usually leads to a collapse of lust and the need for lengthy recovery period.

Playing the multiple orgasm game can be one of the most enjoyable solo sex practices. For one thing, you can make it last for hours, an intimate exploratory adventure between just you and your cock. You'll learn to love it in brand new ways, to enjoy a kind of buddy-buddy companionship that few men know, and that certainly ranks up there with the very best sexual pleasure that any human being has ever experienced. It's a game of teasing to the point of sweet torture, a gentle, lovely sadomasochism in which you pleasure yourself while refusing to bestow upon you the *ultimate* pleasure until you choose.

Begin with whatever stroke you like, but be sensitive to the earliest sensations of pending orgasm. Then, back off to slow, gentle movement. Let the feeling build gradually, with you in control, rather than arriving like an explosion.

Eventually, you'll reach a point of intense pleasure, and equally intense hunger to go further. You're approaching the point of inevitability, of no return, where the involuntary ejaculation will start—and within a few seconds end. This is the point that separates the men from the boys. Be satisfied where you are. Don't go for the biggie—don't even see how close you can get to the edge at this point. With practice, you'll be able to come up to the very brink without plunging over, but not at first.

Now that you're here, try to relax all your pelvic muscles completely. Imagine yourself floating in this altered state of consciousness.

There are several ways to control orgasmic intensity and climax, and you should experiment to find which are best for you. E. Douglas Whitehead, M.D., a director of the Association of Male Sexual Dysfunction in New York City, says that one method that has been reported effective in delaying ejaculation when it's threatening, even when you've ceased all movement, is to contract the ischiocavernosus muscles, the same muscles you contract in stopping urination or defecation. But keep in mind that our bodies are very individualistic in the ways they respond; another man—with first-hand experience—was quoted in a New York magazine as advising the opposite: "Once a man reaches the point of no return and knows he is about to ejaculate, he should go limp (i.e., relax all muscles)." Find out which works best for you.

Use your thoughts to control the high. If you want to get closer to the edge, think sex. If the ejaculation threatens to overwhelm, a good technique is to fasten your mind on the color blue, which is known for its calming value. You'll be astonished at how easy it is with practice to back off, then creep up, back off, creep up repeatedly using mental control.

The same results can be achieved physically, based on what you've learned in earlier chapters. When you grab your penis in your fist and pound down toward the scrotum firmly, for example, the skin of the organ is tightened, applying tension to the glans. That increases the intensity of sensation, and in itself can produce orgasm and ejaculation in some men. It can bring you, in slow and controlled fashion, right to the edge and over. With careful timing, you can shorten or ease the stroke slightly to reduce the tension while preserving the "preliminary" orgasm.

Another method that has been found effective by multi-orgasmic men: Those who have developed the ability to powerfully contract the ischiocavernosus muscles, as recommended by Dr. Whitehead, learn to contract them rhythmically, mimicking the thrusts of intercourse without actual movement.

"I start by pumping it hard—you know, grabbing it in my fist and really going at it," explains one man. "Then, as soon as I feel the first tingling, I slow down, just hold my dick in two fingers, my thumb and the next finger, but I still slide up and down the shaft. Then, when I get real close, I take slow strokes, up by the head, maybe bump the head each time with my fingers, but I don't pull down hard, because if I tighten the skin behind the head I can lose control and shoot too soon. It's an art form. And I'm an artist."

Others simply shake their penises as though flicking moisture from its tip. Still other message the head between their fingers. Only by experimenting will you find the best technique for you.

If there's such a thing as a graduate course in the art of the multi-orgasm, it would probably be a full orgasm with complete ejaculation, lasting three or four times as long as a typical orgasm, very satisfying and yet allowing almost immediate continuation of sexual activity—the sort of experience reported by the 28-year-old man from Mesa, Arizona. It is, with the exception of the ejaculation, identical to all descriptions of the female orgasm. We might call it the graduate course in the androgynous orgasm. And, while rare, it is certainly within the realm of achievement for many men.

It's done by approaching the very brink of inevitability—and then allowing yourself to slip (not plunge) over. By pulling the skin tight on your penile shaft, it's possible to put a maximum amount of tension on the nerves of the glans, or penile head. Beyond the stimulation, *don't move*. Concentrate your entire mind on the feeling. Urge it on.

When you know ejaculation is unavoidable, relax all muscles. With practice, you can even reduce or eliminate the spasms of ejaculation, and without them the orgasm will continue much longer than usual. As you learn to completely eliminate these contractions, you'll experience wonderful orgasms with the possibility of continued erection and libido.

No, you won't be a total master of the multi-orgasm overnight. But as social psychologist Carol Tavris says, "Remember that the multiple is 90 percent a matter of expectations and learning. Old habits can be broken and control can be established through masturbation and intercourse. Excitement and curiosity will get you there."

And practice. Practice. *Practice*. But of course if you didn't have that in mind in the first place, you wouldn't be reading this book!

Chapter 11
Heightening Hunger Through Abstinence

FROM THE moment we're sufficiently coordinated to bring our pudgy little hands in contact with our penises, the negative conditioning begins: Don't touch that. Penises are dirty. Sex is dirty."

Later, we get the modified version. The rabbi says, "Never during the woman's menstruation." The minister warns, "Only with your wife—unless you're a TV evangelist." The priest says, "There's nothing dirty about sex. We're just too good for it."

Buddhist monks take it further than other religious leaders. When they feel sexual desire in their loins, according to *The Encyclopedia of Religion* (1987), they're taught to envision a dead body, blue, swollen, worm-eaten, with all its intestines, excrement, bile, pus, fat, mucous and urine. That should be effective in destroying the sex drive of any man, unless he happens to be a sadistic scatological necrophiliac.

The consistent message: If sex is not exactly evil, it certainly isn't clean and pure and good.

Given that perspective, it follows that he who would be truly saintly must forsake sex. Early Christian followers of Origin and others did so in the extreme, removing their genitals for Christ's sake, thereby making solo sex—or any sex—a real, although not impossible, challenge. The Skopts of Russia did the same, removing first their testicles and then their penises for God—who, one would think, would not have put them there in the first place if He wished us to remove them.

But not all celibacy is for so truly deranged a reason. Today, many people are saying no to sex for non-religious reasons. Most of them already understand lust first hand, and have experienced sexual pleasure. They've outgrown the myth of sex-as-evil. Yet, they're committed, at least temporarily, to sexual abstinence. Some of their reasons are naive, others silly. Still other motives might prove of great interest to you in enhancing your own sexual capacities, especially in terms of *achieving the psychic orgasm.*

Here are some of the reasons men give for at least temporary sexual abstinence:

A Return to Innocence. Daniel Gold writes in *The Encyclopedia of Religion,* "appearing as the original state of man born of the spirit, celibacy in Christianity, as in other traditions, promises innocence—eternal childhood in the Lord."

In other words, some guys blame sex for the fact that they've become adults, faced with the complex responsibilities and decisions that maturing requires. They believe that by denying their sexuality their lives will grow simple and pure again, and they'll be able to cope more effectively.

Curiously, it just might work—but it has nothing to do with a return to innocence. In fact, as you'll see, the key might be just the opposite, an increase in sexual tension.

Gaining Control of Lust. Some men think that by denying themselves sexual fulfillment they can reduce the intensity of their sex drive. Which is about as bright as going on a fast in order to reduce hunger. According to church historian Henry C. Lea, early Christian priests made the same mistake. Boasting their virginity and their strength to resist any temptation, they hurled themselves into situations that would have made a eunuch potent, even bathing naked with beautiful women. The result was licentiousness that would have put to shame any libertine, and the destruction of many newborn infants in order to protect priestly reputations.

Elevating Sex to a Higher Moral Plane. Howard and Martha Lewis, who direct Human Sexuality, the computer sex education service to which I referred earlier, quote a young man in their book *The Electronic Confessional:* "Sometimes I was sleeping with three girls at a time, and even engaging in mate-swapping and group sex....

"Recently this whole way of life has gone sour. Sex is no longer the kick it used to be. I've decided not to have sex again unless it's with a woman I want to marry, or at least care about very much."

According to Dr. Joel Moskowitz, a psychiatrist with the Resthaven Psychiatric Hospital and Community Center in Los Angeles, a growing number of young people are experiencing what he calls "secondary virginity." To them, casual sex has become not only unsatisfying, but disillusioning, leaving them feeling depressed and empty.

Women may suffer even more profoundly from the disappointments of casual sex. Betty Holcomb told her story in the December, 1985, issue of *Essence,* and after interviewing women who have forsaken sex with men for short periods, she concludes, "Temporary celibacy may be one of the healthiest choices a woman can ever make in her sexual life."

Note this important point: regardless of the definition offered by some theologians, celibacy is not synonymous with sexual abstinence—and Betty Holcomb is apparently referring to abstinence rather than celibacy. Celibacy is "the condition of being unmarried, usually by reason of religious vows." It comes from the Latin *cælebs,* meaning unmarried. Technically, one can be celibate while living with a woman, or man, although the general sense is that one who is celibate does not have sex with other people. One can certainly be celibate and enjoy solo sex regularly, however.

Abstinence, however, is the willful rejection of the very existence of an appetite. To abstain is to hold back from fulfilling a desire or craving. Sexual abstinence is the willful refusal to satisfy sexual craving.

While the person forsaking sex for innocence or mastery of the sex drive may choose total abstinence, those trying to overcome casual sex impulses might well become celibate—avoiding sex with other people while continuing to enjoy less frequent but more satisfying and meaningful sexual pleasure alone.

Focusing Attention on Other Goals. In the 1970's Mitchell Ditkoff decided to intensify his efforts at what he calls "finding myself." He joined an experimental subculture of several men who had recently also become abstinent. Although skeptical, he writes in the December,

1986, issue of *Glamour,* "...all I found was a sincere desire to create an environment for nurturing personal growth."

For some people, it's a workable and satisfying alternative, at least temporarily. The U.S. Census Bureau reports that a larger percentage of Americans are living alone than ever since the early part of the century—about 41 percent of all marriageable people are now single. Peter Stein, professor of sociology at William Patterson College of New Jersey, says, "I see people who choose singlehood as developing a viable alternative lifestyle where the focus may be on career, education, relationships, political activities, community involvements—a number of other issues."

To Build Sex Tension. Now, *this* is the reason we're interested in celibacy and abstinence. Imagine a typical Tantric ritual: A naked man squatting on his knees, penetrating a naked woman, her legs and arms embracing him, the two humming a chant. Neither moves for 20 minutes, after which, neither having achieved orgasm, they separate.

In Tantric worship, the goal isn't to suppress sexual desire but to actually encourage it, then to use that pent-up passion in religious zeal. It's the same principle in Chinese Taoism, and no doubt in the licentious rituals of ancient Rome.

The point is this: There is no more intense driving force in normal human beings than sexual hunger. In fact, it just may be the *only* driving force, as anthropologist Robert Briffault wrote in *The Mothers,* way back in 1927:

"Every aspect and product of human cultural and mental evolution can be directly or indirectly brought into relation with the reproductive impulse when its operation is diverted. Social restrictions and cultural associations have diverted the operation and defused the energy of the sexual impulse, thus giving rise to highly complex emotional states..."

Here's the reason that even those who seek a more child-like, simple life can find it through sexual abstinence: denying our sexuality intensifies all other aspects of life. Unless it becomes a distraction in itself, it increases the energy for pursuing other goals. It enhances introspection. Temporary abstainers report that they've learned for the first time since childhood that there's more to them than genitals. Some report actual euphoria as a result of freedom from passion.

Others claim that they've found meaning in their lives after their sacrifice of sex activity.

But the point, as Briffault wrote, is that euphoria isn't, in fact, the result of freedom from passion. Euphoria *is passion,* expressed non-sexually. Intensity and meaning are simply redirected sexuality.

That's important to keep in mind regarding our purposes in this book. If *quality* of sexual experience is more important than *quantity* in your life, then short-term abstinence has a very definite role to play for you. Certainly, most men are like children in a candy store; they'll stuff every pocket, along with their mouths and jockey shorts, indiscriminately with the sweets at hand. A few of us opt for the fresh experience, the unique or the rare, the breathtaking. You are probably among those relative few, or you would not be seeking a higher level of solo sex experience in the first place.

Short-term abstinence is particularly useful in preparation for the psychic orgasm, which can be achieved only through a high state of sexual passion. If you would grade your lust level as a C or lower, you might consider temporary abstinence as a means of recharging your batteries.

Keep in mind that abstinence can be effective as a means of building sexual tension only if it lasts long enough to actually make you want to have an orgasm desperately. It's not enough to say no when you don't feel like saying yes anyway.

The benefit accrues when you *really want to let it happen,* and still abstain.

Many men want an answer to, "How long should I abstain?" That's a difficult question, depending entirely on individual psycho-physiology. If a man would ordinarily have only one orgasm every two weeks, obviously a libido-building abstinence would have to last well beyond that. On the other hand, the fellow who has three orgasms a day might well be abstaining almost beyond endurance by the second day. The way to gauge yourself is this: If you have abstained until you are all but overwhelmed with your preoccupation with orgasm, you have held back long enough.

What sort of an experience can you anticipate? Although no two are likely to be entirely alike, the following detailed account, written by a young reader of one of my books, illustrates well the process of increased sexual tension that you can probably anticipate if you choose to abstain from sex. For that reason, although it is quite detailed, I'm including it here in full. The following is quoted verbatim:

THE JOY OF SOLO SEX

I didn't plan to give up sex for a week. I wouldn't have thought it possible. For 10 years I'd been having three orgasm a day on average—some days one, other days five. Nancy, my first wife, had been born with enough lust in her heart to match the passions of any man, and our marriage had been a marathon of inventive lovemaking punctuated by violent arguments. The quarrels eventually came to dominate, and we divorced while still in our 20's.

Early in April we separated. The following month I left to visit a friend in Tallahassee.

The day I left was the beginning of my sex fast, although I didn't know it then. Although I realize that virtually any amount of sexual activity, from one orgasm a month to 35 a week, is considered normal [as my book had pointed out], the machinery of my body had been purring along nicely for 10 years, since my late teens, on a more or less ritualistic orgasmic schedule. The longest lapse had been during a hospitalization of four days.

After the emotional roller coaster of the previous six months, zipping along the highway in that beat-up old Volkswagen Beetle was intoxicating in its unfettered freedom. The first night I stayed in the Charlotte, North Carolina, YMCA, wandered the streets, ate, slept. I reached Atlanta by noon the next day, decided to stop there, to explore—I felt as positively alive to life and as eager for adventure as a child.

The following afternoon I reached the Tallahassee horse farm where my friend, Ken, worked. I chugged down the dirt lane under the great boughs of eucalyptus and live oaks decked in Spanish moss, the stables and corals in the misty distance. I'd been on the road three days, and hadn't once thought of sex.

154

That changed immediately. Ken worked at a breeding farm specializing in Pasos, a South American import with a natural, unusual lope. As I drove into the stable area, I discovered Ken's boss pulling on one old stallion's semi-hard dick. When it finally firmed up to a respectable 30 inches, the trainer urged the doddering stud with a glorious bloodline into action, even helping the beast find the target.

Bestiality is not one of my scenes, though, so I don't really count that as thinking about sex.

Later, Ken and I sat naked in his living room, sweating in the heat of a Florida night in late spring, sipping beer and bringing each other up to date on our lives for the past 13 years—it had been that long since, as friends in our mid-teens, we'd seen each other. I told him about Nancy. He told me about Marge. She'd just dumped him, and it was his fault. He cared about her, even loved her, but couldn't say those words. He'd always been a little flaky about expressing his feelings, even as a kid.

The following night, the fourth of my trip, Ken hit the sack early. He had to start feeding the horses and cleaning stalls at five in the morning. Alone in front of the TV, relaxed and half intoxicated, I glanced down across my nude torso to watch my dick doing a gentle dance with no thought or effort on my part. Slowly it spasmed its way to full erection. I remember smiling, amused that this could be happening to a man in his late 20's, without any sexual thoughts or physical stimulation. I wondered how far the process would go. Would I ejaculate that night in a wet dream? Would I have an orgasm?

In fact, I had a nap, right there in the chair, and awoke the next morning, long after Ken had left. I wondered if my pole had been flying high when he'd passed through the living room to shut the TV off and go to the kitchen, or when he'd sat at the table a few feet away sipping his coffee. I'm an exhibitionist at heart, and the idea excited me.

In fact, beginning that morning, a great deal began to seem sexually stimulating. That was the start of the fifth day, and I awoke as I'd fallen asleep the night before, hard as a rock, my hand clutching my dick. I could have gotten off so easily then, still half asleep, the desire rising, unrestrained by an alert mind. But I stopped.

Now that I really want it, I thought, why not see if I can resist for a whole day? I'd never even thought about restraint before, but here was a fantastic possibility: actually getting a sex kick out of having no sex. The feeling in my gut that morning was warm, glowing, secure, invigorating. I felt more together, more concentrated, and I liked it.

I got dressed immediately, first slipping into my undershorts, which I rarely did when wearing jeans. I didn't want to be distracted by the feel of my dick flapping around in my pants, by seeing the bulge against my left thigh.

For this one day I wanted to be psychologically cockless. I wanted to feel sexual in the rest of my body, see sex wherever else it might be, not just between my legs.

And that's what happened. It wasn't like those hippie acid trips of the 60's, and yet it was certainly an altered state of consciousness. A horse cantered across a field tossing its head, and the flow of its mane was feminine and inviting. The puffed breast of a swallow, the graceful veil of Spanish moss, the sweat trickling down Ken's muscular torso. My own straining muscles, the smell of

156

my body, the scent of leather. The distant groans of mating alligators in the swamp. The tall, phallic pines.

I was simply filled with it all, not with lust and desire but with a warm, unifying assurance that sex isn't something we *do*, but something we *are*, that we are every moment celebrating our sexuality with all the world around us.

That night, however, sexual need became concentrated in His Excellency La Dong. For one thing, my balls were beginning to grow sensitive to touch.

The reason for this, as you explain in your book, is that the testes continue to produce sperm whether or not it's expelled from the body, and eventually this accumulates in the seminal vessels, backs up in the vas deferens and eventually starts pushing out the walls of the factory— the nuts. That tingling discomfort focuses a man's attention on his sex organs, which is supposed to lead him to relieve the tension.

I had also been preoccupied with sex all day, even if in a more diffused sense than usual, as I described. I did not think once of sex *acts,* or people and sex, just the fact that I was sexual, but there is nothing quite like devoting an entire day to being conscious of your sexuality.

That night, after my shower, there was just no way to keep the fact from Ken that I was sporting a hard-on. Actually, he got a kick out of it, although he didn't respond in kind. I told him about my experiment, and he laughed heartily for the first time since I'd arrived.

"So you're not gonna beat off till tomorrow morning, huh?" he chided, and proceeded to recite in detail the horniest episodes of his life. From there, we started sharing fantasies. All during that time, my cock was at full attention. I could even feel an occasional spasm of the prostate, a process that, once underway, might lead irreversibly to ejaculation and orgasm without any manual stimulation whatever.

Finally, I told him my all-time favorite fantasy. "I've gotten off on this one ever since we were buddies in Smitty's barn," I told him. "You were going with Cindy and I was with Caroline at that time. I'd get this scene in my head—we took both of them up there in the loft, and we all got naked. We were side by side, you and me, you on Cindy, me on Caroline. Maybe you and I would look at each other, even hold hands, and that's how we'd make out with our girls."

Reliving that fantasy got me so high I was ready for anything. Come on, Ken, I was thinking, take hold of it. Give me what I need. Whack me off. I'll love you forever. For a minute, I thought I saw a look in his eyes, and now that I'm older and not afraid to admit some things about myself, I realize that Ken and I probably did have a crush on each other when we were kids, and at that minute there in his house in Tallahassee, we felt that attraction again. He kept staring at my rigid cock.

Then he looked up at me. His own dick was sticking out, and he was blushing. But we were both too homophobic to act on our feelings

"Better take care of that thing," he said, and went to bed.

Later that night on the sofa, the heat flooding all through me, every part of my body feeling more alive than I ever remembered it, I finally made up my mind that I would not quite yet throw away this natural high of unbearable hunger by having an orgasm. I would continue to resist the fire inside.

The next day I worked myself silly tossing bales of hay and shoveling shit out of stalls, and fell asleep early that night. For the first time in years, I had dreams of breasts, vaginas, warm torsos—and Ken's naked body. Twice I awoke on the verge of orgasm, thrusting against the mattress, and, with stubbornness of will I hadn't realized I possessed, I stopped and rolled onto my back.

The next morning Ken and I said good-bye, and I started back to Pennsylvania by way of Charlotte. I suppose it's a miracle I didn't get arrested—I drove naked, pulling my shorts up from my ankles to make the necessary stops, and while car drivers couldn't observe anything, a number of truck driver tooted their approval as I chugged past them in the old VW sporting my cock in all its glory.

By the time I checked into a room in the Charlotte YMCA that night, I knew the time had come. It was the seventh day. The seminal fluid accumulating in my prostate was causing serious discomfort. My body had conditioned itself to ejaculate fluid three times a day, and now was storing 21 gobs of the stuff somewhere inside me. I needed emptying.

What's more, I was absolutely losing touch with reality. I didn't make a habit of driving naked all day. Sexual frustration will do that to a person. As you said in your book, it might even lead to sex crimes. I believe that.

That night in ritualistic fashion I lay my dick over the bathroom sink and stared at it. I thought of Ken and me and the girls in the loft of Smitty's barn, he and I such close friends that we had pledged to die for each other, the first soul mate of my life. In my fantasy, he watched my ass move up and down over Caroline, and I watched him, his chest pressed against Cindy's large, soft knockers.

The rest was up to my body. I never touched my cock. Yet, it performed mightily, rising steadily. The prostate began spasming, first tiny, sporadic contractions, then, involuntarily growing more rhythmic, more forceful.

The rest, as they say, is history.

This account is of particular interest because it shows just how intensely sexual desire an build in a man who is used to having daily orgasmic release. In this case—and I hope in yours—that final ejaculation comes about not through physical contact but psychic tension.

This man has given in a classic example of the ultimate orgasm, *the psychic orgasm.*

That is the subject of the next chapter.

Chapter 12
Psychic Orgasm - The Ultimate High

THERE ARE fantasies.

And then there are realities of the mind.

"I got better and better at sex pictures. I could begin with a couple of people, someone else and me, some other people without me, any combination was suitable, and have them have sex. I had... two men having sex with me, some women and a man having sex with me, sometimes this bunch of people would be having sex and I would be one of them."

Rey Anthony, the woman who wrote *The Housewife's Handbook on Selective Promiscuity,* is not describing simple fantasies. She's talking about vivid, *real* experiences. During them, she's in another world. It's a reality, an altered state which has been termed mystical, a self-induced hypnotic trance. In fact, it's both—and those who have known it say it's the ultimate sexual high.

"I built up the sexual sensations in my body," Anthony continues, "all over my body, and, half-asleep, half awake, I reached a climax.... It had been so fascinatingly real—I thought I must have been masturbating—but I wasn't. I had a climax just by creating the sensations in my body and achieving the intensity necessary to reach a climax."

Men, too, have reported psychic orgasms. "The first time was when I was in my late 20's," says Allen B., a former pastor of a Baptist church. "I got out of the shower and dried off and then went over to the sink. There was a large mirror on the wall behind it. I laid my penis on the counter so that it hung over the sink. I pressed tight up against it and just stared at my organ. I didn't move or touch it or anything, just stared at it, just kept staring until it was the only thing in the world. I could feel the blood throbbing into it in rhythm with my heart beat.

"I just relaxed, drifted into a kind of twilight zone. The beating of my heart was actually masturbating me, and I was just there watching, not even a part of it. Even the penis wasn't part of me anymore. I knew it was going to happen. I just knew. The orgasm started so slow and nice, just going through me, all over my body—maybe that's what a woman's orgasm is like. It was the greatest thing. Not 10 or 20 seconds, but minutes, two or three at least. Even when it was over I just stood there weak and in a daze for awhile."

Allen describes the spontaneous orgasm, the ultimate psychic orgasm, which occurs without any physical stimulation whatever. Apparently that's rare in the Western world. Two highly respected sexologists—Clelland S. Ford and Frank A. Beach—in their book *Patterns of Sexual Behavior,* devoted only one sentence to the spontaneous orgasm: "There are a few women and men who say they are capable of inducing a complete sexual climax in themselves by indulging in sexual fantasies."

Elsewhere, it's long been a different story.

R.E.L. Masters writes in *Sexual Self-Stimulation* that "Psychic self-stimulation procedures are taught in the Orient and have been highly systematized by a few erotic-religious sects."

Those men and women who frequently achieve such orgasms describe them as other-worldly in their intensity,

duration and effortlessness. Many say they are a profoundly spiritual event. That's virtual heresy to many West-
erners—linking sex and religion. Yet, says Masters, there
exist "certain Oriental sects, where masturbation is in fact
one means of effecting mystical union with the deity."

"In the Madras section of India," writes sex therapist
Jane Dobbs Butts in the *Journal of the National Medical
Association,* "there is a popular cadence (raga) which
literally means 'sexual intercourse' (orgasm) and 'union
with God' simultaneously." The Indian yogi-scientist
Pandit Gopi Krishna has written several books based on
his philosophy of "erotic mysticism," an outgrowth of
Tantric Yoga, in which lovers embrace in coitus but remain
motionless while worshipping together for half an hour or
more.

When an American or European discovers the psychic
orgasm, it's almost always by accident. There are no
books on the subject—this is probably the first chapter
ever written about it. Yet, *it has been described*—rarely—
in the medical literature. Psychotherapist Helene Deutsch
tells of a case:

"Her orgasms were extraordinarily gratifying; according to her description, she experienced them in full consciousness, but had the impression hat she was not
herself; she felt as though she were living in a different
world, 'as though in heaven.'"

Others have written of orgasms that trigger "a more or
less intense clouding of consciousness," which "shut out
conscious thinking," or which, as Kinsey found, culminate
"in extreme trembling, collapse, loss of color, and
sometimes fainting of the subject."

Physiologically, here's what seems to happen to bring about the psychic orgasm: The individual's concentration on sex becomes so intense that his body interprets the sexual excitement just as it would an external challenge calling for a "fight or flight" response. That leads to the release of large quantities of catecholamines, particularly norepinephrine and dopamine. These neurotransmitters sensitize the nervous system to greater and more rapid response. They also make the nerves extremely sensitive to physical sensations—such as the pulsing of blood through the penis. You'll recall that, in the case of Allen B., the Baptist pastor, he actually felt the rhythmic flow of the blood engorging his organ. To the uninitiated, that might seem a farfetched fantasy, but when one understands the psycho-physiology involved, it becomes a perfectly natural phenomenon for most men to experience.

Ultimately, researchers such as Julian M. Davidson, professor of physiology at Stanford University, believe that it is this stimulation of the neurons of the septum, a part of the limbic system at the top of the brain stem, that triggers orgasm. (Orgasm, remember, has nothing to do with either erection or ejaculation in terms of areas of the brain involved in control. Each is a separate process controlled through its own mechanism. Under certain conditions, men can experience orgasm without erection or ejaculation, and can ejaculate without orgasm or erection.).

Here's what those who experience psychic orgasms have in common. Take time now to analyze your own sexuality and determine whether you have psychic orgasm potential.

A Joyful Love of Sex. That's not as easy to come by as you might think—it's not the leering, lustful "I gotta get laid tonight" craving for the basic fundamentals of the act, although that's part of it. More importantly, it's absolute freedom, deep down in the unconscious, from any guilt or shame associated with sexuality. To put it in the terms of one mystic, "Every time I have an orgasm, the heavens celebrate."

But sex for those people is not merely genital. They can lie naked in bed with arms outstretched and legs spread and feel a sexual tingling in their abdomens, chest, arms and legs. They understand what it is to have sexuality flowing through them.

Now you are beginning to see why I included that lengthy testimonial in the previous chapter of the man who imposed upon himself a week of sexual abstinence. Only then was he able to attain an overall, rather than strictly genital, sense of sexuality.

A Sophisticated Sexual Appetite. Although there are moments of urgency when they'll settle for the quick thrill, they're willing to forego the immediate hamburger in order to develop a greater appetite for the steak later. They don't exhaust their psychic potency with the sexual equivalent of nonstop nibbling on junk foods. They allow the sexual tension to build up, anticipating the banquet—the psychic orgasm.

Even the abstaining gets to be a powerful high, as we discussed in the previous chapter.

Vivid Imagination. Ultimately, the psychic orgasm is the product of auto-suggestion, or self-hypnosis. And auto-suggestion requires imagination. Discussing hypnosis in general, Nicholas P. Spanos writes in *Psychiatry,* all subjects who responded well to "hypnotic" suggestion "constructed imaginary situations which, had they objectively occurred, would be expected to produce the behavior called for by the test suggestion."

A woman who was unable to raise her arm said, "I *imagined* that there were all kinds of rocks tied to my arm. It felt heavy and I could feel it going down; I couldn't stop it."

Another could not keep her arm from rising: "I *imagined* that my arm was hollow and somebody was putting air into it..."

Time and again the researchers used such expressions as, "*Imagine* you are holding something heavy in your hand." "I want you to *imagine* a force acting on your hands to push them apart..." "*Imagine* that your hands are two pieces of steel that are welded together so that it is impossible to get them apart..."

Writing in *Archives of General Psychiatry*, psychiatrist N. Lukianowicz, M.D., tells the story of a middle-aged man who was capable of standing before a mirror and imagining himself transformed into a woman. Eventually, with the vividness of a real experience, he would see a naked man "stepping out of the mirror, with his penis stiff and erect, trying to embrace me..."

Here's an example of joyous love of sex that surpasses even the limits of individual gender. The man continues, "After a few minutes of looking at myself in the mirror, I sort of lose myself and forget about the whole world. Everything becomes unimportant, far away and forgotten, and my whole attention is concentrated on my own image reflected in the mirror.... It is a sort of sweet intoxication, a sort of half-dream, during which I do everything almost unconscious, like an automation... Somewhere at the back of my mind there is a vague notion that I then masturbate, but at the same time I see him bending over me and pushing his big stiff penis into my body, as if I were a real woman... I wake up from this trance just after I release my sperm and have only a vague and patchy recollection of all that happened during my intoxication."

Ability to Become Completely Absorbed. The first step into an altered sexual state is to embrace the fantasy or mood. It's not enough to think about it, even in detail. In fact, forcing yourself to concentrate is exactly the wrong thing to do. It's the intellectual approach, and the intellect is typically the antithesis of passion.

The term preferred by researchers Duke Tellegen and Gilbert Atkinson is *absorption.* Writing in the *Journal of Abnormal Psychology,* the doctors define absorption as "a 'total' attention, involving a full commitment" of the senses—the body, the imagination and all thoughts—to a single object.

"Objects of absorbed attention acquire an importance or intimacy that are normally reserved for the self and may, therefore, acquire a temporary self-like quality," they write. "These object identifications have mystical overtones, and, indeed, one would expect high-absorption persons to have an affinity for mystical experience..."

A New York City commercial artist tells this story of his psychic orgasm: "It was really late—maybe two in the morning. My girl and I were driving back to the city from the Jersey shore. She'd fallen asleep next to me, and I was getting sleepy myself, so I unzipped my pants and began playing with my penis.

167

"I began thinking of this girl I'd seen on the beach, really built and practically naked in her bikini. I wasn't thinking about having an orgasm—it would have been too messy. I was just getting myself high.

"I got high, all right. I got so that I was in a daze. For more than an hour I kept having this orgasm, this different kind of climax, not as intense but broader, if you can understand what I mean. All over my body. And I didn't have to do a thing, maybe a tug every 10 or 20 seconds, just concentrate on that girl."

While most men are turned on by action-type fantasies, those who report psychic orgasms usually are stimulated through becoming totally absorbed by a single object, often a part of their own bodies or that of another.

One woman described by R.E.L. Masters begins by gently massaging her clitoris. Gradually, she drifts into a trance-like state and feels her clitoris growing larger and larger, becoming a penis. She becomes *aware* of masturbating this huge penis with her hand, can actually *feel* the cock in her palm, *feel* it enclosed within her fingers. In that state of reality, she continues until reaching a glorious ejaculation.

A college junior reports visualizing two breasts hovering over his face. They're softly illuminated in the pink light, but everything else is covered with black velvet. so absorbed does he become in his fantasy that he can *feel* the skin against his cheeks as the breasts caress his face.

Among the small minority of men who experience psychic orgasms, many, both gay and straight, become absorbed in the image of a huge erect phallus—an ideal self. Disembodied hands touch it, lips caress it, and as absorption grows more intense, the psychic orgasm begins.

It is there for the experiencing—by any man or woman who is truly not ashamed of his or her sexuality, who is willing to say no to lesser thrills for a time, and is capable of setting free his or her imagination.

Now, let's get down to nuts and bolts, so to speak. Let's assume that you do have a joyful, guilt-free love of sex, a sophisticated sexual appetite, a vivid imagination and the ability to become completely absorbed. (This entire book has been constructed like a pyramid to help you progress, step by step, to the point at which you are ready to achieve the psychic orgasm, so, if you have any problems with it, you should go back and reexamine the chapters to see where you need more practice. And I'll give more information in this chapter on how to increase the depth of your absorption and imagination.)

But before I go on, I want to make certain that every reader knows exactly what we're talking about when we use the term "psychic orgasm." Some of you might think I'm being redundant, but not long ago I wrote the only article ever to have appeared in an English language publication for laymen on the subject of the psychic orgasm, and as a result I received many letters, some of which I'll include in this chapter. Through that response, I learned that I had not clearly defined what a psychic orgasm is. Let me do that here and now:

It is an orgasm produced *entirely* though mental or psychological or emotional processes. Although physical stimulation of the penis might take place preceding orgasm and the organ might be held passively during climax, physical stimulation is completely absent during the build-up of physical sensations and the orgasm itself.

True psychic orgasms are every bit as intense and pleasurable, and of precisely the same nature as the orgasms you have every day, although they may be more or less intense, more or less satisfying, just as ordinary climaxes vary in the pleasure they produce.

All right, let's do it.

You already know how to create a more real than live sexual fantasy. (If you don't remember, go back now to chapters 8 and 9 and review; you must master that before you can achieve this.) You'll recall first relaxing your body through stretch exercises, then relaxing the mind with a *Perfect Peace Scene.* Finally, you allowed the scene to dissolve into a solid, relaxing color that filled your entire mind. You'll go through those steps again now in approaching the psychic orgasm.

Now, when your mind is completely blank, you can go in any of three directions:

First, you can create a lust-filled fantasy, preferably one you haven't used for solo sex before. The freshness of a new fantasy will make it more compelling.

If you choose the fantasy approach, limit the scope of activity. In other words, make it a single activity rather than a whole series of involvements. The reason is that the more complex your fantasy becomes, the more likely you'll get intellectually involved in the storyline, whether you intended to or not. This should be as much as possible a thought-free and completely emotional experience.

Call into play all the senses. Without actually thinking about it, smell the perfume or cologne, the body odors, the sheets. Feel the skin and muscles, the moisture, the sweat. Look carefully at the details of the anatomy. Really *see* in your mind's eye all that exists before you. Hear the moans, taste the bodies.

Even those of you who think you don't have the imagination required might well prove quite capable if you have typical sex drive, for that can go a long way toward stimulating what imagination you do have to work along sexual lines. Just give it time. Enjoy the experience wherever it takes you.

Those of you with good imaginations will find yourselves so engrossed or absorbed in the scene that you'll have an auto-hypnotic experience. It's the same experience that mystics have when emotionally they leave their bodies and therefore feel no pain when lying on a bed of nails, or when they're transfixed into a vision of heavenly splendor. It's believed by some authorities that out-of-body experiences are also related to this phenomenon. It is nothing more or less than concentrating, imagining, so intense that for all intents we actually exist in the fantasy scene we've created.

Second, you might put that intense concentration to envisioning a static—or photograph-like—picture. Allen B., whom we discussed earlier, fixated all his attention on his erect penis as he saw it reflected in the bathroom mirror. For some men, that can be profoundly erotic. Others concentrate on the image of their entire bodies, but the most common static subject of concentration, both among men and women, seems to be the erect dick.

Third, you might concentrate on body sensations. The most masterful practitioners of the psychic orgasm generally prefer this approach. That's because, almost from the beginning, there are pleasurable physical sensations involved, sensations that others miss because their concentration is elsewhere.

If you want to try experimenting with this approach, start by stretching out nude on a bed and proceeding to become completely relaxed physically and mentally. When the mind is cleared of all thoughts, concentrate on being touched by imaginary fingers. *Feel* the tracing of fingers along your inner thighs. Keep concentrating on the sensation until you actually begin to *feel* it, a light, tingling touch.

Feel your lower abdomen being sucked inward, toward your spine. This area, about two inches above your pubic bone, is known to the practitioners of Tantric yoga as the Seat of Desire. As the abdomen is pulled inward by an inner vacuum, think of that energy as being transferred into your genitals.

Your whole body grows lighter, floating on waves of erotic pleasure. Feel the tingling and tightening of desire as your breath quickens. Allow yourself to breathe rapidly.

As you become more absorbed in the erotic sensations you're feeling, you'll begin to notice the most distant tingling of orgasm. Let it come. It may take a long while, but that is one of the unique beauties of the psychic orgasm. It won't pound you into oblivion. It will simply overwhelm you in the most soft and flowing and yet fulfilling way. As you sink deeper and deeper into the experience, there will come a point when you will know that you're going to have an orgasm.

This is a fine example of the truth of the Biblical verse, "All things are possible to them that believe." When you are truly certain—not pretending to be, but genuinely—that you will have an orgasm, you will.

Here are the testimonies of a few men who have experienced this rare pleasure:

I never touched myself, not once. But in my fantasy, a hand was massaging my cock. I actually *saw* it, and the thing that amazed me was that I *felt* it. I swear it's true. I felt the hand sliding back and forth on me slowly, hardly touching me, the touch was so light, and I got higher and higher. When I felt the orgasm and knew I was shooting, I opened my eyes and looked at myself. I was gushing all over the place, and for a second I couldn't believe no one was touching me."

"This won't make any sense, but it worked for me. I kept staring at my dick and imagining it was getting bigger and bigger and I was getting smaller. My whole life was in my dick, everything, my brain, the works. I was a big cock, that's all, lying on the grass in front of George M. Cohen's statue in Times Square, and the people were so freaked out that they just kept staring at me in awe while I shot gallons of cum."

Ultimately, whether you take the fantasy, fixation or sensation approach, it will be necessary for most men to end up concentrating on the building sense of orgasm. One man has written that, at the first tingling, he begins saying aloud, "Yes, yes! Yes, It's coming!" The words confirm the reality of the experience, and his rapid breathing helps physiologically to bring the orgasm to fulfillment.

I want to close this chapter by quoting portions of three detailed letters from men who have had various experiences with the psychic orgasm. The first man hadn't actually intended to have the experience. He was watching a sex video and "I got my wang out and held it but did *not* jerk off." He remembered reading my article in which I described the possibility of, in his words, "having an orgasm without whacking off, a feat I considered impossible (unless you are sleeping—I have had a few wet dreams) for me, but I decided to try anyway. I pulled down the skin as far as I could and held the base of my dick firmly in my hand while concentrating very hard on the video. Every few seconds I would jiggle it a little, but not up and down, and as time went on, I felt the sensation build up, closer and closer to climax. It took about an hour of this until finally I ejaculated. I don't think I could have done it without the video, and I really had to concentrate hard on it."

If you've been reading this book for more than case histories, you know exactly why this guy had such a difficult time of it. First of all, the tone of his letter makes clear that he was using his head instead of his feelings, his emotions, trying "hard" to achieve a goal, not relaxing into an experience. Secondly, he was relying on an external source of sexual stimulation. Certainly that might work for an adolescent, for whom erotic videos are a new experience. But there is no external erotica as effective as that generated by your imagination, simply because you were not manufactured on an assembly line and your erotic turn-ons are, in some very real and profound ways, uniquely yours.

With the information in this book, however, this fellow can become expert at psychic orgasms.

The second letter comes from a 32-year-old musician from Anaheim, California. His name is Jerry:

"My orgasms (when properly set up and with the right partner) are absolutely earth shaking. When it occurs I truly feel not on this earth, definitely an out-of-body experience. I lose my breath and shake for a long time, as if in total collapse. I almost feel like fainting. My partner doesn't know what to think, of course, so I just have to assure him I'm okay. Just let me come back to earth gradually.

"I can much relate to the things other 'psychic orgasmers' have in common—freedom from guilt, non-genital sex—more mind sex, tingling, sex rushing through my veins sort of feeling, a slow build-up of sexual potency, strong imaginative 'reality' and complete absorption.... I have a strong affinity for mystical experiences also, which I feel must have something to do with it."

While there is nothing in the above letter that rules out this man's experience as a very intense but ordinarily achieved climax, he himself described the experience as a psychic orgasm. I have accepted his word for it. Therefore, I can surely empathize with his sex partner, who apparently does little more than to sit there while the letter writer without explanation is suddenly convulsed in a seizure of ecstasy.

The final letter comes from a 28-year-old New York City man:

"I seem to feel most comfortable with myself when I'm nude. I enjoy being naked tremendously whether indoors

175

or outdoors. When at home in my apartment, few minutes go by that I am not fully naked enjoying letting my body breathe freely....

"I love to look at myself naked in the mirror and sometimes masturbate while looking at my reflection in the mirror. Every morning and evening when I dress and undress I always take the time to enjoy my naked presence in the mirror. It has often puzzled me as to how I can get such a kick out of seeing myself nude! I must state that I am a fairly good-looking guy but I am not muscular and I am by no means a 'stud' or a 'hunk.'

"During this time of watching myself in the mirror I drift off into a daze exploring and feeling every part of my body, most often without actually masturbating my penis. The sensations most often overwhelm me....

"When I lie in bed naked I feel a very intense tingling sensation throughout my body that is very difficult to put into words. Feeling the soft sheets against my naked body is incredibly arousing and I get an immense satisfaction from this without stroking my penis or ejaculating. I most often fall asleep on my side holding onto the pillow like it were a body next to mine. I like to use a very slow thrusting hip motion of intercourse in order to fantasize about a man and woman having sex using my vivid imagination to picture the couple in a similar position of coitus, imagining the sight of the man's erect penis sliding slowly in and out the woman's vagina and watching the man's hips flex as he goes through the physical motions of intercourse while penetrating and withdrawing from the female partner.

"I am able to use my imagination in such a way as to achieve the gratification of having an orgasm myself without ever ejaculating from just the mental image of the couple engaging in sex. I frequently use the male image of someone I have recently seen nude at the health club. My fantasies are almost never of men having sex with each other. I am able to create a wave of sensations throughout my body just from letting my mind go into a daze and think about what is in the man's head while having his penis inside a vagina that is wet and tingling with excitement. I have engaged in intercourse with a few women, so I do remember what it feels like.

"My sexuality is in no way confined to the genitalia. I do feel that I do have sensuality and sexuality flowing through every part of my body. I believe that I first realized this fact after I got naked outdoors for the first time. The first time was on a skinny dipping expedition at a deserted creek. Getting naked outdoors seemed like a good idea because there was the aura of being a bit naughty and also the possibility that someone might see me. I will never forget the feeling and the heat from the sun and the light summer breeze as it engulfed my entire body! It was then that I realized that sexuality was not confined to the penis alone, although it was an important part. Swimming nude is something I think every male alive should experience. The feeling of being free of a swimsuit, no matter how skimpy, and allowing the water to run across your buttocks and feel your dick and balls gliding gently through the water is as great as having an orgasm."

An amazing number of people in our society believe that the ideal of male sexuality is the beer-swigging, shit-kicking macho. In fact, that stereotype isn't even in the running. The men who know the most about sex, and who get the most out of it, are sensitive and honest guys such as this letter writer.

THE JOY OF SOLO SEX

"Often I find that I'm having 'sex' merely by being in the presence of certain people. It no longer matters whether they are male or female, what they look like, how they live, what they do....I am always 'making love' with those around me in accordance with their capacity to enter energetic rapport. It does not require words, or even knowing one another."

—Richard Moss, *The Black Butterfly*

Epilog
The Healing Power of Sex

FOR MORE than a quarter of a century now, I have written about sexology, including solo sex. In the old days, I used the more common term, masturbation, but I abandoned that word because solo sex, as we've seen, can involve a great deal more than self-stimulation of the genitals. What's more, I quickly realized that the word masturbation represented not merely an *act* but an *attitude* toward that act. Even those who held a frankly positive attitude toward sexual self-pleasuring spoke and heard the word "masturbate" with negative feelings. It equated with childishness, deviance, embarrassment, immaturity—not at all what I had found the practice of solo sex to represent. It was time to applaud and extol solo sex, to openly praise it as a gift of God, perhaps the greatest pleasure He's bestowed upon us.

Now that the evidence is in, now that the common people have ceased relying on the irrational dictates of sexually celibate—therefore, perverted—clergy, and have begun relying upon their own good common sense in matters sexual, the truth about erotic self-love can be told and understood—but the word "masturbation" can never lose its negative baggage.

So I wrote and I lectured, and to my surprise many men responded positively, using the very word I had rejected, giving it a new, liberating meaning. Here are just a few of the letters I received in response:

"Congratulations to Dr. Litten for his uninhibited view of masturbation. Litten demonstrates that we need not feel guilt over an action we enjoy. My own masturbatory experiences have progressed from school urinals to masturbating in front of my partner, so that she will know how to better please me sexually. In order to become completely sexually liberated, we must first stop feeling guilt over solitary sex."

—I. W. N.
Minneapolis, MN

"Thank you for publishing the article, "In Praise of Solitary Sex." I thought it was terrific! I thought I was a bit strange when I masturbated but after reading it, it made me relieve tension. Sex is a great thing!"

—Washington, D.C.

"Thank you, Dr. Litten, for writing a very interesting and honest article about solo sex or masturbation. So many men are so shy and closed-minded about the subject; whereas you brought it 'out of the closet.' I belong to a Jack-Off Club; but all 200 members aren't gay. There are many 'straight' men and bi-sexual men who just enjoy doing it without any hang-ups or 'getting it off' in front of others. Your article was refreshing and nice to know that masturbation *isn't* strictly for gay men.

"As you say, despite denials, all guys have and still do jerk off. In Nancy Friday's book on *Men in Love,* she gives evidence of boys starting in at six or seven and continuing into married status.

"Personally I adore my modest seven inches of staff as it is beautifully shaped with a dandy full crown. Every pre-dawn erection gets kneaded, baubled and massaged for the joy of feeling it. I use body lotion after bathing and the crown jewels get special attention to keep them nice and smooth.

"All in all, a cock is a gorgeous piece of machinery and I'm sure every honest bloke loves and prides it without any reservations."

—T. D.
Boston, Mass.

"I had to laugh when I read the line, 'Honk if you Masturbate!' As every moment on the highway would sound like a wedding procession if everybody had a bumper sticker like that. I also remember many days when I couldn't wait to get home and take hold of it!

"Slamming your ham, choking the chicken, tossing off, conversing with Rosy Palm or whatever you'd care to call it is most definitely fun and surely practiced by almost everybody. Bravo, Dr. Litten..."

—G. A. F.
Oak Lawn, Ill.

"I find that masturbation is salvation of marriage and from other misunderstandings and problems, so that men do not have to go to burden their wife or go to strange women for 15-20 minutes of sex joy.

"Not only teenage guys or adult single guys, but also married men like to enjoy solo sex, especially alone in a hotel room on a business trip, reminiscing of youthful first feelings."

—K. S.
Redlands, California

Those are just a representative few of hundreds of such letters I've received over the years. In a nutshell I've said, "Solo sex is not merely to be tolerated or endured, but to be exalted and pursued with enthusiasm." When readers and audiences responded so eagerly, I was surprised. Then I wasn't.

For I realized that sexual self-love is as fundamentally necessary to most of us as eating and sleeping and loving others. When these people responded they were saying, in effect, "Thank you for telling me that this pleasure, which is so necessary to keep my body and mind working right, doesn't make me evil or dirty."

Through every stage of our post-pubertal life, solo sex is central to both our emotional and physical well-being. A boy of 12, who until now has been non-orgasmic but has been having disturbing and messy wet dreams (nocturnal emissions) which he does not understand and a startling, pleasant tingling that never fully resolves itself into pleasure—upon advice of friends, he takes his tiny erect penis between his thumb and forefinger and messages as they suggested until suddenly his whole world is blasted to pieces in a nuclear bomb of such violent, uniquely overwhelming pleasure that, for a while, he could not move if he had to. Now he understands something very profound...not consciously, perhaps, but something nonetheless that becomes and integral part of his existence. This is what my dick is for, why it's been getting big all by itself. This what it means to be male rather than female. He is grateful for this dick, the source of this great feeling. It may be that he is on some level even thankful to God for it, unless of course he has been brainwashed into feeling that sex, and therefore his dick, is evil. He is, perhaps for the first time in his life, aware of his gender and proud of it. He will now swagger as a young man, roll his hips, walk with his hands in his back pockets, stick out his chest. He owns a dick, and whether it's a big one or a small one, it's just the right size to make him feel damn good whenever he wants.

I'm saying that the penis and the pleasure it brings is the most significant single factor in early male adolescent life. And, apart from genetic programming, the degree of masculine development that youngster will achieve depends to a great degree on just how frequently he makes sexual love to himself. There is overwhelming evidence that sexual activity leads to increased production of the male sex hormone testosterone, which is responsible for genital growth, muscle development, deepening of the voice, growth of hair on the body. (See Robert Bahr's excellent book on the male sex hormone, *The Virility Factor,* for an exhaustive discussion of the subject.) In fact, although I do not expect any physical education instructors to say so, young body builders would probably do well not only to pump iron but also their penises regularly if trying to build muscle.

And what is true of adolescents is also true of adults. The man who is highly active sexually all his life will remain so well into old age. People have always supposed that, and in the 1940's Alfred Kinsey confirmed it. More recently Dr. William Masters and Virginia Johnson have made similar findings. A highly active and continuing sex life in the younger years is related to continuing high levels of sexual performance throughout old age. And if that activity is solo sex, it seems to be as effective as if it were coitus.

Now at last there's a good explanation for why that's true. Sexual activity stimulates the male gonads, the testicles, to produce greater amounts of testosterone.

Among the first to report that was endocrinologist C. A. Fox. He described a 38-year-old man who for two months took blood samples from his own body before, during and after coitus with his wife. By analyzing the blood for hormone levels, he found that sexual activity caused a dramatic increase—sometimes as high as 50 percent.

To men who had already done similar research with laboratory animals, Fox's report came as no surprise. They had found that both bulls and rabbits showed a significant testosterone increase following sex activity. In fact, merely placing a male rabbit in a cage containing a female rabbit in heat is sufficient to increase his testosterone blood levels tenfold!

Monkeys react similarly. Four of them placed in separate one-third acre pastures by researcher Robert Rose enjoyed for two weeks the perfect life—plenty of food, water, open space and a harem of female monkeys.

Almost immediately their male hormone levels began moving up from their ordinary or baseline levels. Ultimately the increase was from 109 to 247 percent, a phenomenal rise.

Exactly what do increased blood testosterone levels mean as far as functional sexuality is concerned? In the animal there is no question about that. As hormone levels go up, so does the libido, or sex drive, or plain old lust.

Scientists have a very well developed theory to explain that in both animal and man—the problem in humans being that research ethics forbid injecting young studs with testosterone and sitting back to watch how sex-crazed they become.

We recognize sex stimulants through our senses. We see an attractive, desirable sex partner. We feel the softness (or firmness) of the body, its touch on our skin. We hear the voice, smell the stimulating odors.

In animals, these are probably the exclusive sources of erotic stimulation. In man, his imagination (fantasies and such) also play a part. But the senses remain even in humans the major source of original erotic stimulation.

The senses immediately telegraph their erotic messages to the brain, and in particular to the hypothalamus, an area of the brain in the center of the skull about ear level.

The importance of the hypothalamus to overall body function cannot be exaggerated. That's because it functions in a sense as a combined airport and railroad terminal. Messages "fly" into it through the nervous system. Those messages are "unloaded" in the hypothalamus and shipped locally to other parts of the brain and throughout the body on a slower acting "railroad" of chemical secretions.

In fact, that is what hormones often are—chemical secretions resulting from stimulation of the nervous system. It's the hypothalamus which, after receiving signals from the nervous system, sends the orders to the various endocrine glands to secret hormones.

That is precisely what happens in the normal man when he responds to something sexy. His hypothalamus immediately sends the message to his testicles to begin producing testosterone at higher levels.

Yes, even the *idea* of sex can have the effect of raising testosterone levels. That was shown in a study of 16 healthy young men divided into two groups. Group B was treated to three and a half hours of children's cartoons. Group A watched hardcore pornography. (Don't you sometimes wonder why *you* are never paid to participate in these studies?)

Blood samples taken every 15 minutes for both groups, and electrical devices measuring the number of erections, showed the predictable. Bugs Bunny and Silverster Pussycat failed to stimulate increased hormone rates among the men watching the cartoons. On the other hand, all the men watching the sex flicks had erections during the three and a half hours, an all but two of them had dramatic increases in testosterone.

Once the hormone is secreted into the blood by the testicles, a circular pattern begins. The blood carries the hormone to the brain's sex center, also located in the hypothalamus. There it triggers a desire for sexual activity.

(Incidentally, according to many researchers, including Helen Kaplan, Ph.D., M.D., sex desire in both men and women is triggered probably exclusively by the male hormone testosterone. In men it often increases libido, in women it *always* does so. So dramatically do women react to testosterone that for them it is probably the only true aphrodisiac in existence. It is normally produced in small amounts by the woman's ovaries, and hyper-sexuality in women, along with body hair, is a symptom of an ovarian tumor causing the gland to be hyperactive.)

As the sex drive increases, the hypothalamus orders the testes to continue to step up its hormone production. Ultimately, the unsatisfied sex drive can reach a frenzy, particularly in animals, who have not been socially conditioned to control their passions. Eventually the male may become violent if his sex release is frustrated.

After orgasm, the sex desire vanishes in most males. Still, it will take more than an hour for the hormone levels to begin lowering.

As most men grow older, there is a slow but definite decrease in testosterone production, along with a waning interest in sex activity. As I have already stated, that is not a foregone conclusion, and many men continue to be sexually active. Certainly part of the explanation is genetic, but, according to Clyde E. Martin, Ph.D., who interviewed 451 men from 45 to 84 years old for the Gerontology Research Center in Baltimore, "Both mechanisms [heredity and sexual activity] undoubtedly contributed to the maintenance of individual differences [in later levels of sex activity]."

Solo sex is the simplest way of assuring continued sexual activity. Few writers have so eloquently sung the praises of solo sex as did David Cole Gordon in his book *Self-love* (Verity House, 1968). He makes the point that many people have no partners to maintain a sex life with, and, without sexual self-pleasuring their sex lives would be crippled in middle age and would probably not recover in old age when it can be of special importance in easing loneliness.

But Cole goes further, arguing that society should actually aggressively encourage solo sex—for these reasons:

"Masturbation furnishes an invaluable outlet which permits sociopaths and psychopaths to act out their overheated sexual fantasies which they might otherwise stage as sexual crimes, violating not only innocent victims but the social more and morals. It [solo sex] acts as defense for society, protecting it against highly sexed individuals with strong instinctive cravings and inadequate ethical and sexual inhibitions. Many of our sexual crimes are committed by precisely this type of individual who refuses to resort to masturbation because he regards it as unmanly..."

Cole argues that abandoning erotic self-love can actually lead to suicide.

"One theory is that the individual feels that he is giving up life itself when he abandons his self-stimulating activity. As we have seen, what he is asked to give up, or relinquishes voluntarily, is, in effect, life's peak experience itself. It is perhaps the most intense unification experience known to man, who may never have had either a theoretically more satisfying heterosexual experience, or even a homosexual relationship. He gives up the essence of life, and possibility of the repetition of the climactic moment of unification when he is one with himself and the world and his problems are resolved. People who are so troubled by, and yet put such a high premium on the act of masturbation, probably have not experienced unification any other way or through any other activity, and indeed are too inhibited to make it with a member of the other or even their own sex. They are giving up life itself if they renounce their solitary practice, and are reduced to the gray depressing round of their normal existence."

As long ago as the early 1960's, when a large percentage of medical doctors still condemned masturbation, Dr.

Earle M. Marsh, coordinator of Allied Health Professions at the University of California Medical Center, actually prescribed solo sex for some of his patients. Although Marsh practiced obstetrics and gynecology, which means that most of his patients were women, what he had to say applies to both genders:

"My patients, most but not all of whom are women, tell me invariably that they derive great relief and pleasure from masturbation. I advise them to continue to practice it, and not to worry about it in the least. It produces relaxation, release from tension, cheerfulness, and a sense of ease.

"Without it, some people who do not have adequate sex contact with partners might explode.

"I also recommend masturbation for teenagers, as a release of their sexual energies, and I even go so far as to say that it cuts down juvenile delinquency. I find considerable support for this among my colleagues."

In fact, many authorities, including Dr. Gordon, cited earlier, argue that solo sex might very well be at least a partial answer to the increasing number of young people who become juvenile delinquents. The reasoning isn't in the least complex. Humans are biologically programmed to begin reproduction usually between the ages of 12 and 14. That means that their bodies become capable of producing eggs that can be fertilized and sperm that can do the fertilizing. But it means a great many more things, as well, one of which is that, along with the *capacity* to reproduce, there is a *drive* to do so.

If that drive did not exist, it's unlikely that any of us would go through the otherwise rather ludicrous gymnastics of sexual intercourse. We conduct that highly pleasurable ritual because we are *driven* to it, knowing even as virgins in some instinctive way that we absolutely *must* copulate, or do whatever else we can to reach orgasm.

Now, we know for certain that among both young people and adults some have little sex drive and others have an all-but-obsessive passion for orgasm. If social mores condemn masturbation as a sick, childish, sinful or disgusting act, the adolescent male might well feel compelled to impregnate a woman instead. And if no woman is available, the building sexual tension of highly sexed individuals *must still be released.*

Here is something I would ask you never to forget:

Sexual tension will always find release, either through its intended route of coitus or masturbation, or through perversion that may be sexual, or social. It may entail rape or child abuse. It may entail murder, vandalism, senseless violence. But there is no exception to the fact that sexual drive will express itself even if it must masquerade to do so.

Someone will point out that many people are celibate, leading saintly, sexless lives. My response is that many such people have a physiologically limited sex drive. Often, their hormone levels are quite low. And limited sex drives can be sublimated, expressed in deeds of kindness which bring a pleasure that is sometimes obviously erotic to the trained observer.

Apart from such individuals, frustrating sexual expression is like sealing the lid of a pressure cooker and turning the heat up. I would seriously like to see some in-depth

190

experiments conducted among hard-core juvenile offenders in which they would be indoctrinated into the knowledge of the God-given goodness of the orgasm and encouraged to give themselves as many of them as possible each day for several weeks. I am as convinced as I have ever been of anything that, as long as they continue to release tension through this means, these youngsters will remain as docile and cooperative as any other member of society.

Dr. Gordon, cited earlier, adds this to the list of benefits from solo sex: "Among the minor though important benefits assigned to onanism is a frequent aid to the sleeplessness caused by the physical restlessness and psychical irritation resulting from insufficient sexual gratification. The release of tension through orgasm frequently relaxes a person sufficiently so that he can sleep..."

What a wonderful world it could be if the typical family physician routinely had the courage to treat insomnia by saying, "Have one orgasm and call me in the morning."

It is time—no, it is long past time—to recognize erotic self-pleasuring with the joy and gratitude that expresses its crucial importance in our lives on every level. Let no one ever again apologize or feel shame or embarrassment at being discovered at solo sex or suspected of it or for admitting to enjoying it. Let those of us who are honest in our sexuality go on the offensive.

What this country really needs is a few bumper stickers in praise of solo sex—such slogans as:

I Can Do It Myself, Thanks.
*If **You** Won't Do It For You, Why Should I?*

Pleasure Thyself
Meet My Favorite Sex Partner
Up With Solo Sex
Solo Is a Four-Letter Word

It's been said that the typical human uses only about 10 percent of his brain power. I've written this book in part because I think we use about the same percentage of our erotic capacity.

That's to say that our capacity for erotic pleasure—the intensity of it as well as the frequency—has hardly been tapped. The primary reason for that is the shameful, guilt-ridden attitudes with which Western society has enshrouded all sex. It is an abnormal and potentially highly damaging attitude at best, and one that leads to perversion and suicide at worst.

If I've been able to help you to free yourself from this sexual damage and embrace your sexuality and your potential for a new level or orgasmic pleasure, then I have done precisely what I have set out to do.

I'd like to hear about your experience. Perhaps I'll even get to include your testimony of joy in another volume. Although the press of time and volume of mail prohibits personal responses, you can be sure I'll read carefully and file for future use every letter. Write to me at the following address:

FACTOR PRESS
Post Office Box 8888
Mobile, Alabama 36689

All the best!

ABOUT THE AUTHOR

Through books, newspaper columns, lectures and more than 500 feature articles, Dr. Harold Litten (a pseudonym) has provided advice on sexual matters to millions of men and women. A recognized authority on sexology, he considers this present volume in many ways the summation of his philosophy of sexual health.

Dear Reader,

When we began FACTOR PRESS in 1990, we had one purpose: to publish a book on Solo Sex that would help men of all ages, both gay and straight, to embrace their sexuality as good and even sacred. It was, in a sense, an evangelical effort—we preached the cleansing, healing power of orgasm.

Today, the book you've just read has become a cult classic. The first copies, though crudely typeset and printed, are collectors' items. And a fraternity of sorts has come into being.

That's led us to publish *CELEBRATE The Self Newsletter—CSN.*

Here's what *CSN* is all about:
*Readers' solo sex
  games and experiences.
*Harold Litten on "Sex
  and Your Health"
*My own column, "God
  of the Body"
*Bargains and Rip-offs
  in Erotica
*Book Reviews
*Recommended books,
  products at 15%-65%
  discounts
*Reader experiences in Celebration of the Self
We carry no advertising. We keep subscribers' names confidential.

Won't you join us in this grand, new Adventure!
One year (four issues) for *$12.95.*

Send check or money order to:

In celebration,

Robert Bahr
Publisher

FACTOR PRESS
P.O. Box 8888
Mobile, AL 36689
VISA, MC, phone 1-800-304-0077